KUMON READING WORKBOOKS

KU-443-684

5

Reading

Table of Contents

KUMON

Vocabulary
A Rooftop Garden

1

Date   /   /

Name

Level ☆

Score   /100

1 Read the following passage. Then answer the questions below.

Last summer, Maria and her mother moved from their house in the country to an apartment building in Chicago. Chicago was very different from their town in Vermont. Maria really liked some things about the city. Chicago had many different kinds of restaurants and the people were also more ①_____ than they were in her small town. The food in the city was ②_____, but Maria missed her house and backyard in Vermont. During the summer in Chicago, she had to go down the street to the park if she wanted to play outside.

Maria had never seen such tall buildings before she moved to Chicago. Even her apartment building was tall. Maria's mother told her that this was because cities were packed ③_____ with people. Fewer people lived close together in ④_____ places like where they used to live. The only way to give so many people a place to live was to make buildings very tall. This seemed strange to Maria. While their building was tall, their apartment was much smaller than their house in Vermont.

Maria knew her mother liked living in the city, but she could tell that her mom also missed having a backyard. Her mom had always gardened in their yard, and now that spring was here, she would have no place to plant a garden. Maria wondered if they could turn some of the space on their deck into a garden. Her mom said it wouldn't get enough sunlight for the plants.

(1) Complete the passage using the vocabulary words defined below.   5 points per question

delicious	very pleasing or agreeable, especially to sense of taste
diverse	different, having variety
rural	from or in the country, often near farmland
dense(ly)	describing something that has many things or people close together

(2) Answer the questions below using words taken directly from the passage.   10 points per question

① Where did Maria and her mother move to from the country?

Maria and her mother moved from their house in the country _____

_____.

② Why are the buildings in Chicago so tall?

The buildings are very tall because it is the only way _____

_____.

③ Why did Maria's mom say they couldn't turn their deck into a garden?

Her mom said they couldn't turn their deck into a garden because it wouldn't get

_____.

Read the passage. Then answer the questions below.

One day, Maria was on the elevator in her apartment building when she noticed her neighbor, Mrs. Garcia, carrying a gardening shovel and a bag of soil. Maria wondered how Mrs. Garcia was able to garden in the city.

"My mom used to grow the most delicious vegetables, and I know she misses her garden now that we don't have a yard," said Maria.

Mrs. Garcia laughed. "I'll show you," she said.

Maria thought that Mrs. Garcia would take her to the park, but instead she pressed the button for the roof. When the door opened, Maria was surprised to see that densely placed gardening plots lined the roof.

"A rooftop garden!" said Maria.

Mrs. Garcia told Maria that for a long time the roof was just an empty space. Then some of the people in the building asked the owners to turn it into a community garden. The building owners liked the idea because the plants not only helped to keep the air clean, but they also helped to keep the building cooler during warmer weather.

"I plant flowers in my own plot," Mrs. Garcia said, "but you would be surprised by how diverse the plants are up here. Some people grow vegetables just like your mom. You can do some of the same things in the city as in more rural areas. You just have to be creative!"

(1) Why does Maria's mother miss her garden?

Maria's mother misses her garden because she used to grow _____

_____.

(2) What did Maria see when the elevator door opened?

Maria saw that _____ lined the roof.

(3) Why are the plants in the garden diverse?

The plants in the garden are diverse because Mrs. Garcia grows flowers, but _____

_____.

(4) What are the two reasons that the building owners like the garden?

The building owners like the garden because the plants help _____

and also help keep the _____ weather.

(5) What does Mrs. Garcia think about living in the city?

Mrs. Garcia thinks that you can do the some of the

same things in the city as in _____

_____.

Do you live in a tall building?

Vocabulary
Keith's Election

2

Level ☆

Score

Date   /   /

Name

/100

1 Read the following passage. Then answer the questions below.

Keith's Aunt Deb is on the town council in High Falls. The people in High Falls have voted for Aunt Deb to represent them three times. Every two years, Keith puts up posters and passes out brochures as part of Aunt Deb's long ①_____ for the spot on the council. He has always listened when Aunt Deb argued about the issues in her ②_____ with the other candidates.

Keith told Aunt Deb that his class at High Falls Elementary was going to have an ③_____ for the school government this month. Aunt Deb was very excited. She thought Keith should run for president just as she did when she was in school. Keith was not so sure. The elections at his school were not usually very exciting. Most of the time, the most interesting issue being discussed was whether the cafeteria should have more pizza days. He also wasn't so sure he had a chance to win. Even if he did, he was not sure what he would do once he was class president.

Aunt Deb thought this was really important. Aunt Deb believed that everyone should show an interest in ④_____ in general. She pointed out that since Keith had always helped with her campaigns, she could now help him too. She could help with posters and give him tips on his speech. Keith decided that this was a good idea. He told Mr. Pratt, the student council advisor, that he wanted to be a ⑤_____ for class president.

(1) Complete the passage using the vocabulary words defined below.   6 points per question

campaign(s)	a planned set of activities, carried out over time, to achieve a goal
politics	the work of government
candidate(s)	someone being considered for an office or position, often political
debate(s)	a discussion of reasons, often public, for and against something
election(s)	an act of choosing by vote

(2) Answer the questions below using words taken directly from the passage.   15 points per question

① How does Keith help his aunt when she runs for town council?

He puts up posters and _____.

② What did Aunt Deb think Keith should do?

Aunt Deb thought Keith should _____ just as she did when she was in school.

2 Read the passage below. Then answer the questions.

10 points per question

Aunt Deb asked Keith what he wanted to focus on in his campaign, but he still wasn't sure. Soon, he was going to have to debate the other candidates. He worried that he wouldn't have much to say.

When the time came to debate, it turned out Keith had something to say. Dara, who also wanted to be president, had lots of good ideas, but she wanted to use the class money for an ice cream day. This would mean there would not be enough left over for the trip to the science hall. Keith said it was silly to spend the class money on an ice cream day. The science hall would be less expensive and more fun. Many of the students had been hoping to see the laser show. Keith thought Dara was a good candidate for president. He believed she would listen to the other kids and make good choices for them, but she was wrong about ice cream day.

After the debate, Mr. Pratt had some advice for Keith. "You made some good points, Keith, but there are other ways to participate in politics without being the president. Maybe what you need to think of is a way to have the president listen to your ideas about the class money." In the class election, Keith was not chosen to be president, but he was glad. He was chosen to be treasurer! He would be in charge of the class money after all, and he could make sure the class went to the science hall.

(1) How did Keith answer Dara's idea for an ice cream day?

Keith said it was _____

_____ when the science hall would be less expensive and more fun.

(2) Why does Keith think Dara is a good candidate for president?

Keith thinks Dara is a good candidate for president because he believes she will listen

_____.

(3) How does Mr. Pratt think Keith should participate in politics?

Mr. Pratt tells Keith he needs to find a way to have _____

to his _____ about the class money.

(4) Why was Keith glad that he was not chosen to be president in the election?

He was chosen _____, and he would be _____

_____ after all.

Do you want to run for class president?

_____

Vocabulary
The Giant Squid

1 Read the following passage. Then answer the questions below.

For a long time the giant squid was thought to be a ①_____ that didn't exist. In stories, the giant squid was a sea monster that attacked ships. Even when giant squid became stuck on beach shores, they were taken for mermen*! But now we know the giant squid is real. No person has seen them in their natural ②_____, but witnesses have ③_____ these creatures above water and sometimes washed up on the shore. Recently, one was even ④_____ and brought onto land.

Just how ⑤_____ is a giant squid? It is one of the biggest animals on earth. The biggest of them can be almost 60 feet long and weigh over two tons. An adult giant squid is about the size of a school bus, but a baby can be as small as a cricket. The giant squid has ten ⑥_____. Eight of these are called arms. Two of the limbs are ⑦_____ and are called tentacles. The arms and tentacles are covered with sharp suckers that help the squids catch food.

Scientists are still not sure what these squid eat or how fast they can swim. Like most squid, they probably live no longer than five years, but even this is just a guess. Scientists still have much to learn about these sea animals. Much of what they know comes from studying the remains of giant squid found in the stomachs of the sperm whales that eat them!

*merman – legendary sea creature having the upper body of a man and the tail of a fish

(1) Complete the passage using the vocabulary words defined below.   5 points per question

habitat	the place where an animal or plant lives
capture(d)	catch
gigantic	very big
glimpse(d)	to take a quick look
limb(s)	arm, leg, wing or flipper of person or animal
legend	myth or story
elongated	stretched out

(2) Answer the questions below using words taken directly from the passage.   5 points per question

① What was the giant squid in stories?

In stories, the giant squid was a _____.

② What is about the size of a school bus?

An _____ is about the size of a school bus.

③ How have scientists learned about giant squid?

Scientists have learned about giant squid by studying the remains found _____

_____ that eat them.

2 Read the passage. Then answer the questions below.

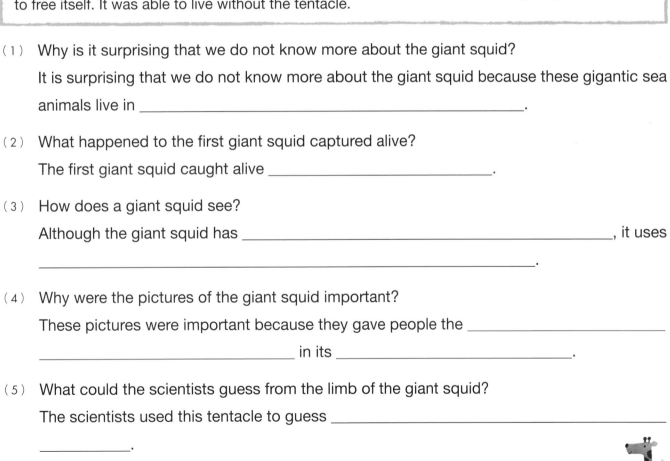

Scientists now think that there are many giant squid. These gigantic sea animals live in most of the earth's oceans, so why do we know so little about them? First, by the time they wash up on the shore, they are no longer alive. No giant squid has lived after being captured. In fact, a giant squid was recently caught alive for the first time, but it did not survive. A giant squid's home is in very dark, cold water which is often thousands of feet below sea level. Researchers cannot safely go into water that deep, and even if they did, they could not see! Although the giant squid has eyes the size of volleyballs, sunlight cannot penetrate the very deep water, and the giant squid must use the light of other ocean life to see.

Recently, scientists have found ways of learning more about the giant squid. A group of Japanese scientists sent an underwater camera deep into the ocean to take pictures. These pictures gave people the first glimpse of the giant squid in its natural habitat!

Scientists learned from the pictures that the giant squid probably swims faster than they had once thought. When the squid got stuck on the researchers' hook, one of its elongated limbs was cut off. The scientists used this tentacle to guess the total length of the squid. They could see from their pictures that the squid was able to free itself. It was able to live without the tentacle.

(1) Why is it surprising that we do not know more about the giant squid?

It is surprising that we do not know more about the giant squid because these gigantic sea animals live in _____.

(2) What happened to the first giant squid captured alive?

The first giant squid caught alive _____.

(3) How does a giant squid see?

Although the giant squid has _____, it uses

_____.

(4) Why were the pictures of the giant squid important?

These pictures were important because they gave people the _____

_____ in its _____.

(5) What could the scientists guess from the limb of the giant squid?

The scientists used this tentacle to guess _____

_____.

Would you like to know more
about the giant squid? I would!

Vocabulary
Sports

Level ★

Score

/100

Date   /   /

Name

4

1 Read the following passage. Then answer the questions below.

When you think of sports, you probably think of popular American games such as football or baseball. However, these games have only been played for a ① _____ time when compared to other sports that have around for thousands of years. Many different types of ② _____ games are played all over the world. Soccer and volleyball are played in the United States but are more popular in other places. Some American games are based on other sports that were played before them.

A game played in one place often ③ _____ a game played in another part of the world. Bats, balls, and nets are used in many sports. The words goal, score, inning and bowl are also used in many sports, but they may have different meanings in each game. Bowling is an ④ _____ of a sport that is played in more than one place. It has different rules and names in other places. In other countries, bowling games are played outside and may use balls instead of pins. Bowling games are played all over the world, including Ireland, Italy, and France.

Baseball came from another sport called cricket. Most people believe that cricket began as a children's game about 500 years ago. Like baseball, cricket is played with a bat and a ball. Cricket is also played in innings, but a cricket match may take days to finish! Cricket is one of the most popular games in the world. Cricket began in England but is played in many places, including India.

(1) Complete the passage using the vocabulary words defined below.   5 points per question

athletic	active, fit, relating to sports
brief	short
example	something used to explain things about a certain group
resembles	looks like or seems like something else

(2) Answer the questions below about the passage.   5 points per question

① What two sports played in the United States are more popular in other places?

_____

_____ but are more popular in other places.

② How are bowling games played in other countries?

In other countries, bowling games are played _____ and may _____

_____ .

③ What sport did baseball come from?

Baseball came from another sport _____ .

④ How do most people believe cricket began?

Most people believe cricket _____

about 500 years ago.

Polo may be the oldest team sport in the world, but it would probably look very new to you if you had never seen it before. Polo was first played 2,500 years ago in what is now Iran. Because it was played by many of the world's kings and rulers, it is sometimes called "The Game of Kings." In some ways, polo resembles hockey. Players use long sticks with heads shaped like hammers to try to score a goal. So why might polo look different from the athletic games you usually see? Polo is played on horseback! The balls fly rapidly, sometimes faster than 100 miles an hour.

Another older sport that might look new to you is played with kites. You probably think of flying a kite as a peaceful activity on a windy day, and in most places, it is. But kites are also used in a rather dangerous-looking game called kite fighting. Kite fighting is popular in Asia and South America. In a kite fight, the kites have sharp objects inside. The players try to force the other team's kite to the ground. A kite fight can be very brief or as long as an hour.

Someday our own games will be played differently. New twists have already been put on modern games. One example is Octopush, a strange game first played in the 1950s. It was based on hockey and was played in a swimming pool with flippers, face masks, and other underwater gear!

(1) What sport does polo resemble in some ways?

In some ways, polo _____.

(2) How do players try to score a goal in polo?

Players use _____
to try to score a goal.

(3) Why might polo look different from the athletic games you usually see?

Polo might look different because it is played _____.

(4) What is the goal of a kite fight?

The goal of a kite fight is to try to force _____

_____.

(5) How long is a kite fight?

A kite fight can be _____ or _____.

(6) What is Octopush an example of?

Octopush is an example of the new

_____ that have been put on

_____.

What unusual games do you know?

_____

Vocabulary Review

5

Level ☆

Score

Date / /

Name

/100

1 Pick the correct word from the box to complete each sentence below.

6 points per question

| limb | elections | rural | captured | legends |

(1) Jane always thought she would end up living in a _____ area because she wasn't fond of city life.

(2) Ping enjoyed reading German _____ because some of them were scary.

(3) Farmer Brown _____ the coyote that had been stealing his chickens.

(4) Free and fair _____ are important to healthy government.

(5) The dog couldn't put pressure on his broken _____, so he limped around on three legs.

2 Connect each word on the left to the correct definition on the right.

5 points per question

(1) delicious ●

(2) candidate ●

(3) habitat ●

(4) gigantic ●

(5) politics ●

(6) diverse ●

● ⓐ the work of government

● ⓑ the place where an animal or plant lives

● ⓒ very pleasing or agreeable, especially to sense of taste

● ⓓ different, having variety

● ⓔ very big

● ⓕ someone being considered for an office or position, often political

© Kumon Publishing Co., Ltd.

3 Complete the crossword puzzle using the sentences below as clues. Use capital letters.

5 points per question

ACROSS

(1) Jim always felt that he ___?___ the president, but he didn't tell anyone.

(2) The homework assignment was a ___?___ summary of the reading.

(3) Through the gaps in the fence, we ___?___ Mr. Steiner's berry patch.

(4) Sports were always easier for my brother, who was more ___?___ than I was.

DOWN

(5) There wasn't much space at the game, and the fans were ___?___ packed.

(6) Most ___?___ for public office take a lot of time and money.

(7) When Shane ___?___ with someone, he gets very red in the face.

(8) The piano player played beautifully with his ___?___ fingers.

Not bad. Not bad at all!

Main Idea & Supporting Elements
Nell's Play

6

Level ★★

Score

Date / /

Name

/100

1 Read the following passage. Then answer the questions below by putting a check next to the correct answer.

Every Thursday, a storyteller named Mrs. Baines visits Nell's class. At first, Nell and her friends thought that Mrs. Baines' visits would be boring. Wasn't story time only for little kids? They soon realized that it wasn't. Nell thought that listening to Mrs. Baines would be like watching a movie without any of the special effects. Once she started though, Mrs. Baines' storytelling was so theatrical, she didn't need anything more than herself to tell a good story. Sometimes the class felt like they were in a theater! Soon, Nell and her classmates were always excited for Thursday.

Every time Mrs. Baines came to class, she told a different kind of story. The first time Mrs. Baines came to class, she told a dramatic story about a ship captain who was lost alone at sea. The class listened very carefully. Everyone wanted to know how the story ended. Some of the stories were fairy tales from other countries. Others were true stories about things that had really happened to Mrs. Baines and her family. Once she told a tale about a selfish lobster that turned green. This story seemed ridiculous at first, but it ended up being very sad. You never knew what you would hear when Mrs. Baines started to talk.

Last week, Mrs. Baines told the class that it was their turn to tell her a story. She didn't care how they did it. They just needed to find a way to tell an imaginative story. Nell planned on writing a script for a play and having her friends perform it for the class.

(1) What is the second paragraph mostly about? 20 points

( ) ⓐ Mrs. Baines told a story about a selfish lobster.

( ) ⓑ Sometimes a story seems ridiculous but ends up being sad.

( ) ⓒ Mrs. Baines tells all kinds of great stories.

( ) ⓓ Some of Mrs. Baines' stories were true.

> **Don't forget!**
>
> The **main idea** is a statement that expresses the most important information in a passage or paragraph.
> For example, the main idea of the third paragraph above is:
> *Mrs. Baines told the class it was their turn to tell her a story.*

(2) What is the main idea for the entire passage? 20 points

( ) ⓐ Thursdays are crazy in Nell's class.

( ) ⓑ Nell tells a story.

( ) ⓒ The children heard a dramatic story in class.

( ) ⓓ A storyteller comes to Nell's class on Thursdays.

© Kumon Publishing Co., Ltd.

2 Read the passage. Then answer the questions below by putting a check next to the correct answer.

Once Nell had written her play, she realized that her plan might not be so easy. Her play had parts for eight actors. She found eight people to be in it, but everyone's schedules were so different that she couldn't get them in one place to practice. She worried that they would not learn their lines in time! Nell told Mrs. Baines about her problem. Mrs. Baines said that Nell might have to find an imaginative way to tell her story.

Nell told her older sister Gina about her problem, and Gina came up with a plan. "I know! We can turn the script for your play into a screenplay for a movie. I can use the camera I use for my film class. You won't have to worry about having everyone practice in the same place because we'll bring the camera to them. This way everyone can look at their lines right before we film them." Nell wasn't sure if this would work because the writing in her play was so theatrical. The story might seem ridiculous and too dramatic as a movie.

Then Gina told Nell she would teach her some simple special effects. Nell agreed that scene two might be interesting filmed upside down so that it would look like the characters were falling. Nell had learned from Mrs. Baines that a good story did not have to have special effects. But then again, Mrs. Baines had said they needed to find their own way to tell their stories.

(1) What is the main idea of the first paragraph?   20 points

( ) ⓐ Nell is worried that the kids in her play are bad actors.

( ) ⓑ Nell is worried that her play will not be easy to do.

( ) ⓒ Mrs. Baines is worried that Nell is not being imaginative.

( ) ⓓ Mrs. Baines is worried that Nell's play has eight actors.

(2) What is the best title for the second paragraph?   20 points

( ) ⓐ A New Plan

( ) ⓑ A Ridiculous Story

( ) ⓒ Learning Their Lines

(3) What is the main idea of the entire passage?   20 points

( ) ⓐ Nell finds a new way to tell her story.

( ) ⓑ Gina will teach Nell special effects.

( ) ⓒ Nell is excited to make a movie.

( ) ⓓ No one in Nell's play can learn their lines.

Telling stories is fun!
Reading them is fun, too!

Main Idea & Supporting Elements
The History of the Map

7

Level ★★

Score

Date / /

Name

/100

1 Read the following passage. Then complete the exercises below.

People have always needed to know where they are and how to travel to where they want to go. Long before we used maps, people used the stars to tell direction. A person who knew where a star was during a certain time of year could use it to travel. Sailors at sea used the stars to help them travel. At sea, sailors saw nothing but water for a long time, and until recently, they did not have radios or communication tools. Instead, they looked up to the sky to help them.

Sailors also found their way with the compass, which uses magnets to determine direction. The compass was first used in China, but later it was used in different parts of the world. The Chinese compass used the magnet to point south. Later, compasses were made to point north. If a sailor knew which way was north, he could easily find south, east, and west. This tool made travel at sea much safer and easier. It is still used by many people today.

A map can also show direction, but it gives much more information, too. People long ago realized that making pictures could help to show location and give directions. Early maps were pictures drawn on animal skins, pieces of clay, and wood. They gave a lot of information, even before the written word and legends* were used in maps. These maps showed things such as settlements, landmarks, and the location of water.

*legend – a table or list that explains the meaning of symbols used in a map or chart

(1) Complete the main ideas for each paragraph in the chart below.   8 points per question

Main Idea	Sailors at sea used ①_____ to help them travel.
	⬇
	Sailors also found their way with the ②_____, which uses ③_____ to determine direction.
	⬇
	People long ago realized that ④_____ or maps could help show ⑤_____ and give directions.

(2) What is a good title for the third paragraph? Check the best title below.   10 points

( ) ⓐ Draw a Picture to Show the Way

( ) ⓑ North, South, East, and West

( ) ⓒ Follow That Star

( ) ⓓ Uses for Animal Skins

2 Read the passage. Then answer the questions below.

The earliest maps were probably drawn in the Middle East. Some of these maps have survived. Taken together, they show what people thought the world looked like at that time. They also show us that people who made them saw the earth as flat. In different places, and over time, the pictures became more detailed and correct. Early on, the Chinese made maps that gave detailed information. The ancient Greeks used their knowledge of math and science to make maps. Greek maps tell us that the Greeks knew the world was round.

From simple pictures, mapmaking has turned into a science. Maps are made by surveying land. In the 1900s, people around the world started to share information to make better maps. Photographs taken from the sky and space also help us see what the world looks like. Mapmakers use these pictures to make maps. Maps are now more correct and more detailed than ever, but since the world is always changing, we will always need new maps.

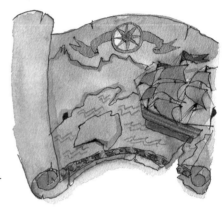

There are many types of maps, but almost all use words and pictures to show what a place is like at the time the map is made. A map usually has a legend that shows what the pictures stand for. Some maps may show the entire world. A road map shows a smaller piece of the world. A road map will have a scale to help you know the distance from one place to another. Other maps may use pictures to show the climate — the temperature and weather — in different places.

(1) Complete the main ideas for each paragraph in the chart below.
10 points per question

Main Idea	Over time, maps became ①_____.
	⬇
	From simple pictures, mapmaking became a ②_____.
	⬇
	Maps use words and ③_____ to ④_____ _____ at the time the map is made.

(2) What is a good title for the second paragraph?
10 points

( ) ⓐ Changing World, Changing Maps

( ) ⓑ Pictures From the Air

( ) ⓒ Sharing Information

( ) ⓓ The Climate Around Us

I think maps are beautiful!

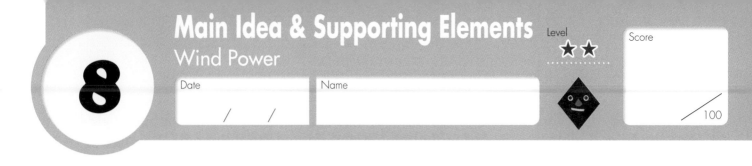

Main Idea & Supporting Elements
Wind Power

8

Date / /

Name

Level ★★

Score /100

1 Read the passage. Then answer the questions below.

Somewhere right now, the sun is making the wind blow. Without the sun, you would not see the wind blow the leaves in the fall, and you would not feel the cold air blow in a winter storm. The sun heats the earth and the air above it, but it does not heat every part of the earth the same amount. This leaves some cool air and some warm air above the earth. Warm air weighs less than cool air, so it rises above the cool air. The cool air then moves in to take the place of the rising warm air. This movement is the wind!

People have used wind as a source of power for thousands of years. Wind can be strong enough to push objects. Wind can also control the direction in which an object moves. Wind does not always blow with the same strength or in the same place, but since it will always blow again, it is an effective supply of power.

Wind power can be used in different ways. If you have ever flown a kite, you have used wind power. The ancient Egyptians first used wind to make sailboats move. Later, people in Asia and the Middle East realized wind could be converted to other kinds of power. They built mechanical windmills, which helped pump water and grind grain into flour. This knowledge was passed on to people in Europe who started to use windmills, too.

(1) Complete the main ideas for each paragraph in the chart below.   10 points per question

Main Idea	The sun makes the ①_____ when it heats the ②_____ above the earth.
	⬇
	Wind can be used as a ③_____ because it is strong enough to push objects.
	⬇
	Over time, people learned to ④_____ in different ways.

(2) Which is the best title for the passage? Put a check next to the best title.   10 points

(　　) ⓐ Heating Air

(　　) ⓑ The Power of the Wind

(　　) ⓒ Kite Power

(　　) ⓓ Windmill Power

2 Read the passage. Then answer the questions below.

A windmill functions by catching the wind in its blades. When the wind blows over the windmill's blades, they turn. Old-fashioned windmills were attached to other tools. Often the tool was a stone used to grind grain for bread. When the windmill's blades turned, a part of the windmill pushed the grinding stone. The stone then crushed the grain below it. Other windmills were attached to a water pump. When the windmill's blades turned, the pump moved water.

These water-pumping windmills were used to pump water from one place to another. Sometimes windmills helped to transform countries by moving water. The country of Holland is famous for its windmills. Holland has so much water that people wanted to move some of it. Thanks to windmills, parts of Holland that used to be underwater are now dry. Moving the water made traveling around the country easier, too. In the United States, windmills were used to bring water to people who lived in areas without many lakes or other bodies of water. Special windmills were even built to pump water from underground. Without windmills, settlers would probably not have been able to farm the frontier.

Though wind power has been less popular in recent years, it is making a comeback. Today's wind machines work much like old-fashioned windmills. They still have blades that turn when the wind blows over them, but unlike old-fashioned windmills, they are not attached to pumps or grinding tools. They are attached to machines that convert wind power into electricity. The electricity is then delivered through electrical lines to homes, businesses, and cities.

(1) Complete the main ideas for each paragraph in the chart below.

6 points per question

Main Idea	Windmills were attached to stones that ①_____ below it in order to make bread and ②_____ that ③_____ water.
	⬇
	Windmills helped to ④_____ countries by moving ⑤_____.
	⬇
	Today's wind machines help ⑥_____ wind power into ⑦_____.

(2) Which is the best main idea for the whole passage? Put a check next to the best idea.

8 points

(   ) ⓐ Windmills helped Americans to farm the frontier.

(   ) ⓑ Wind machines deliver electricity to homes, businesses, and cities.

(   ) ⓒ Windmills and wind machines help people use wind's power.

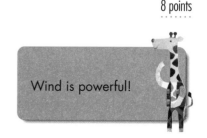

Wind is powerful!

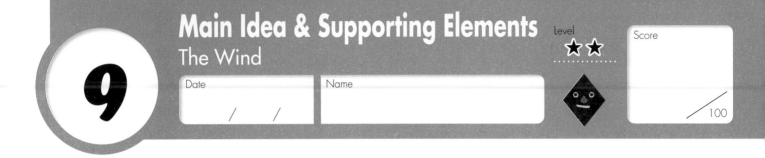

Main Idea & Supporting Elements
The Wind

9

Level ★★

Date   /   /

Name

Score

/100

1 Read the passage. Then answer the questions below.

Most power in the United States does not come from wind, but this may change. Wind is now the fastest growing source of power in the world. Why is wind power becoming popular again?

To understand the answer, it helps to know why the use of wind power declined. It is true that the wind will always blow again, but it isn't always easy to guess when and where it will blow next. People discovered ways to create power that were more reliable. Steam and fossil fuels, such as coal and oil, are very effective sources of energy. For a long time, trains ran partly by burning coal. The gas that powers our cars comes from oil. Coal and oil are burned to create electricity that powers our lights, computers, and TVs.

In the past forty years, we have found that burning fossil fuels is not a perfect way to create power. During the 1970s, there was not enough oil available for energy. People started to realize that wind power might be one way of creating more energy. Unlike oil, wind cannot run out. As long as the sun makes the wind blow, the wind can supply us with energy. Wind power is also a clean energy. Burning oil and coal makes the air we breathe dirty, but wind does not need to be burned to create power. It is a power on its own. Wind power may not be as reliable as fossil fuels, but our ability to catch and use the wind has improved over time.

(1) Read the chart for the second paragraph below. What is the main idea of the paragraph?

20 points

Main Idea	The use of wind power has _____.
Supporting Details	Wind is not reliable. Other sources of energy were discovered. Coal was used to power trains. Oil is used to power cars. Burning coal and oil is now used to make electricity.

(2) What is the main idea of the third paragraph? Put a check next to the correct answer.

20 points

(   ) ⓐ We can run out of oil.

(   ) ⓑ Using fossil fuels for energy creates problems that wind power does not.

(   ) ⓒ Our ability to catch and use the wind has improved over time.

2 Read the passage. Then fill in the charts below using words from the passage.

> We have improved wind machines to catch the wind and convert it to electricity more efficiently. We have also been able to use more wind power by building more wind farms. Wind farms are large areas with many tall wind machines arranged next to each other. Sometimes these wind farms are called wind power plants. They can help deliver electricity to many homes and towns.
>
> Wind farms work best in places that are very windy. It is easier and cheaper to catch wind when there is more of it to catch. These places can be on top of hills, in the gaps between mountains, or on wide, flat plains. Another good place to catch the wind is the ocean. The wind over water is often stronger than over land. Ocean winds are more reliable than land winds. The ocean has no buildings or trees to block the wind.
>
> Wind farms are a very effective way to create electricity, but they have their problems. Wind farms on land take up a lot of space. Many people think the machines are ugly and too noisy. Wind plants in the ocean, or off-shore, mean that less land is needed for wind farms, but off-shore wind plants have problems, too. Builders must worry about hazards like storms and ice. People also worry that wind farms make noise that might scare away birds, fish, and other water animals.
>
> One solution to these problems might be to build flying wind farms high in the air. The winds high in the air are strong and reliable, but for now this is just an idea.

(1) Complete the chart for the second paragraph below.   30 points

Main Idea	Wind farms work best in ①_____.
Supporting Details	Wind farms may be on plains, on hills, or in the gaps of mountains. Wind farms may be on the ocean. ②_____ are more reliable than land winds. The ocean has no ③_____ block the wind.

(2) Complete the chart for the third paragraph below.   30 points

Main Idea	Wind farms have ①_____.
Supporting Details	Wind farms take up ②_____. Some people think wind farms are ugly. Off-shore wind farm builders face ③_____ _____. People worry that wind farms on the water may scare fish.

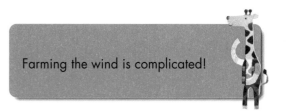

Farming the wind is complicated!

© Kumon Publishing Co., Ltd.

Main Idea & Supporting Elements
The Pyramids

10

Level ★★

Score

/100

Date / /

Name

1 Read the passage. Then answer the questions below.

15 points per question

A   The pyramids of Giza are probably the most recognizable buildings in the world. These buildings tell us much about ancient Egyptian civilization and the beliefs of its people. The Egyptians believed that their kings became gods after their deaths. Their bodies were mummified to protect them for their next life. The pyramids are the tombs where these kings were buried. They were buried with the furniture, treasure, and other things they would need in the next life. The Egyptians believed that if these gods were protected, then the regular people would be, too.
B   These monuments also tell us that the Egyptians knew a lot about building, science, and math. They could not have made the pyramids without this knowledge. For one thing, the rocks the builders used were very heavy. We are still not sure how the Egyptians were able to move them, but we now think that these rocks may have been floated down the Nile River to the building site. The Egyptians used ramps to place the rocks on top of each other. That is how the rocks could have been piled hundreds of feet high!
C   The planners knew that people would want to steal the gods' treasures. They filled the pyramids with secret passageways, extra rooms, and other things to trick thieves, but people were still able to find the treasure. Most of it was taken long before the pyramids were excavated by modern scientists.

(1)   Write the letter of the correct paragraph next to its main idea below.

① (   ) The Egyptians used their knowledge of science, math, and building to construct the pyramids.

② (   ) The pyramid planners tried to hide the gods' treasures from thieves.

③ (   ) The pyramids were built as tombs for the Egyptian kings.

(2)   What is the main idea of the passage as a whole? Put a check next to the best answer.

(   ) ⓐ Ancient Egypt was the first great civilization in the world.

(   ) ⓑ The Egyptians believed that they needed to protect their gods from thieves.

(   ) ⓒ The pyramids of Giza teach us about the knowledge and beliefs of the ancient Egyptians.

2 Read the passage. Then answer the questions below.

A   The biggest and most famous of the pyramids is King Khufu's pyramid, or the Great Pyramid of Giza. It is so famous that it is known as one of the Seven Wonders of the World. It was the tallest building in the world until the Eiffel Tower was built in Paris over 4,000 years later. The pyramid is almost 500 feet tall and was made from more than two million stone blocks. It weighs almost six million tons! Each side is almost exactly the same size. This is an amazing fact because the ancient Egyptians did not have the same building and measuring tools we have today.
B   Khufu began building his tomb just after he became king. It took almost 30 years to build. We do not know much about Khufu, but we do know that he must have been a talented planner. He organized thousands of people, and the resources of his era, to build this monument.
C   We are still learning about Egyptian civilization from this building. In the 1950s, excavators found a wooden boat buried in a pit near Khufu's pyramid. This boat may have been meant to help Khufu on his trip to the afterlife. Khufu's pyramid still holds mysteries that we want to solve. Not long ago, a robot was sent to search behind a sealed door. Researchers hoped to find whether the door was hiding treasure or something else. What did the robot find behind the door? Another door!

(1) What would be a good title for this passage? Put a check next to the best title.   20 points

( ) ⓐ   The Great Pyramid of Giza

( ) ⓑ   King Khufu of Egypt

( ) ⓒ   An Unsolved Mystery

(2) Write the letter of the correct paragraph next to its title below.   30 points

① ( )   An Incredible Monument

② ( )   More to Discover

③ ( )   A Master Planner

(3) Name two details that support the main idea in paragraph C.   20 points

Main Idea	We are still trying to learn more from Khufu's pyramid.
Supporting Details	In the 1950s, excavators found a ①_____ in a pit near Khufu's pyramid.
	Not long ago, a robot was ②_____ _____.

I wonder if there is still some treasure in the pyramids!

Vocabulary Review

Level ★★

Date / /

Name

Score /100

1 Pick the correct word from the box to complete each sentence below.

6 points per question

| civilizations declined delivered scale dramatic landmark |

(1) Isabella was very _____ about things. It was as if her life was a play.

(2) We drove too far because our father didn't check the _____ on the map.

(3) Many _____ have considered cats to be special animals.

(4) Chris was invited to a party, but he _____ the invitation because he didn't feel well.

(5) The newspaper landed in the bird bath when it was _____ this morning.

(6) I can't get lost in my town because the clock tower by town hall is a good _____ that is always easy to spot.

2 Read the sentences below. Then circle the word that is the closest in meaning to the underlined word in the sentence.

6 points per question

(1) Omar wasn't sure if the seat was <u>available</u> or not, but he sat down anyway.

    free   full   heavy

(2) Over time, a caterpillar <u>transforms</u> into a beautiful butterfly.

    opens   falls   changes

(3) Abbie was enjoying her time at the <u>excavation</u>, but she was worried that her team had not found anything special in the dirt.

    dig   party   job

(4) Will had a map, but he was still lost because he couldn't not find his current <u>location</u> on the map.

    street   spot   direction

 © Kumon Publishing Co., Ltd.

3 Complete the crossword puzzle using the sentences below as clues. Use capital letters.

5 points per question

	(6)												
(1) R		L			B								
							(8)						
				(7)	(2)	M			V		
(3) C			M			C			
			G					
	V						
				(4) C		M	T	
(5)		Y			D		
			V			

ACROSS

(1) It's not a beautiful car, but it's ___?___ and it gets me to work every day.

(2) The new and ___?___ version of the computer game was also more expensive.

(3) It's very important to have good ___?___ between teammates. Talking is good!

(4) The ___?___ in South Florida is usually very hot, rainy and humid.

(5) The ___?___ in Egypt are huge!

DOWN

(6) Taping the holes in the tent closed was an ___?___ way to keep the rain out. We stayed dry all night!

(7) Sophie got a good grade on her story because it was ___?___ and fun.

(8) I like ___?___ pencils better than regular ones. They stay sharp!

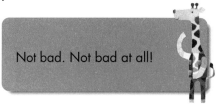

Not bad. Not bad at all!

Cause & Effect
Turboworld 1

12

Date / /

Name

Level ★★

Score /100

1 Read the passage. Then answer the questions below using words from the passage.

10 points per question

Jeremy woke up on Saturday morning and ran to his window. He threw back the curtains and was happy to see a bright sun and nearly cloudless sky. Jeremy let out a cheer. "This is going to be the best day ever. Turboworld, here I come!" he exclaimed. It had all started two Saturdays ago. That was when Jeremy's sister Val had decided that she wanted to go to Sweetwater Park. Jeremy was opposed to this plan from the beginning. He knew that Sweetwater Park would be so boring that he would probably sleep through the whole thing, but Val had raked the yard that week, so their dad had said she could pick the weekend activity. True, after he had swum in the lake and picked blackberries, Jeremy agreed that maybe it had not been so boring, but still he knew that it could not possibly be as fun as Turboworld.

After that trip, he had convinced his father to take the family and some of their friends to Turboworld. Of course, he had to rake the lawn that week, but he knew it would be worth it. However, when he awoke the following Saturday, he could hear the pouring rain hitting his window. They couldn't go to Turboworld that Saturday, so the trip had been postponed until this weekend. Jeremy was so grumpy that rainy day that his father had given him a warning. If he continued to be disagreeable, they wouldn't go to Turboworld at all. Jeremy decided he'd better be patient and cheer up.

(1) Why did Jeremy let out a cheer after opening the curtains?

Jeremy let out a cheer after opening the curtains because he saw a _____

_____.

(2) Why did Val get to choose the weekend activity first?

Val got to choose the weekend activity first because she had _____

_____.

(3) What made Jeremy decide that Sweetwater Park wasn't so boring?

Jeremy agreed that Sweetwater Park wasn't so boring after he had _____

_____.

(4) Why did the trip to Turboworld have to be postponed?

The trip to Turboworld had to be postponed because when Jeremy woke up that Saturday,

he could _____ his window.

(5) Why did Jeremy decide to cheer up?

Jeremy decided to cheer up because his father said if he continued to be disagreeable

they _____.

Read the passage. Then answer the questions below using words from the passage.

10 points per question

"Hurry up!" yelled Jeremy to his family.

"Will you calm down?" exclaimed Val when she sat down at the breakfast table. "There's nothing to yell about."

Jeremy couldn't believe how slowly Val and their father were eating breakfast. Did they want to waste the whole day at home when they could be riding the most colossal roller coaster they had ever seen?

Jeremy had heard about the Twisting Falls of Horror from his friend Mike. Mike had said it was the scariest roller coaster he'd ever ridden, and that afterward, the ground seemed to spin around him for an hour. It was this description of the Twisting Falls of Horror that had made Jeremy beg his dad to take them to Turboworld in the first place. Val was already opposed to riding it. She said she preferred to stay on solid ground, but Jeremy thought Val would have fun if she just tried it.

They were soon on their way to pick up their friends James and Ling. Jeremy was glad that James and Ling both lived close by. This way, they could pick them up quickly and be on their way to Turboworld. But when they got to Ling's house, there was a small snag. Ling's mother said she had to finish her breakfast before she got in the car. They had to wait for Ling for five whole minutes. Those five minutes seemed like an hour to Jeremy, but he decided to be patient. He would need Ling's help convincing Val to ride the Twisting Falls of Horror.

(1) Why did Jeremy yell at his family to hurry up?

Jeremy yelled at his family because he couldn't believe _____ they

were _____.

(2) What first made Jeremy want to go to Turboworld?

Jeremy first wanted to go to Turboworld after hearing his friend Mike's _____

_____.

(3) Why did Val not want to ride the roller coaster?

Val did not want to ride the roller coaster because she _____

_____.

(4) Why did they have to wait five minutes for Ling?

They had to wait for Ling because her mother said _____

_____ she got in the car.

(5) Why did Jeremy decide to be patient?

Jeremy decided to be patient because he would need

Ling's _____
the Twisting Falls of Horror.

Do you like roller coasters?

© Kumon Publishing Co., Ltd. 25

Cause & Effect
Turboworld 2

13

Date / /

Name

Level ★★

Score
/100

1 Read the passage. Then answer the questions below using words from the passage.

Finally, the group arrived at Turboworld, and Jeremy's dad bought their tickets. "Where do you want to go first?" asked Jeremy's dad. Jeremy wanted to ride the Twisting Falls of Horror right away, but James said he didn't want to ride the most exciting ride first because everything afterwards would be boring. Ling wanted to play some games before the rides.

"Roller coasters make me nauseated anyway," Ling said when Jeremy asked about the roller coaster.

Jeremy finally said that it would be okay to wait a couple of hours. After all, the trip had already been postponed a week. What was another hour or two?

Jeremy's dad said they could go on some rides, but they should come up with a plan for what to ride first. Val wanted to ride the Spinning Swans because she knew that at least she would stay right-side up. James really liked heights, so he wanted to ride the Ferris wheel. Ling liked anything fast, so she chose the Racing Turbo Beetles. Jeremy's dad wanted to ride the Bouncing Bumper Cars because he liked to drive. After going on all of these rides, the group stopped for lunch.

They finally found themselves under the Twisting Falls of Horror. Everyone stopped to stare up at the colossal roller coaster in disbelief. "That does look pretty cool," said Jeremy's dad. Val shook her head and watched as a roller coaster car came around the curve above them and then went in an upside down loop, causing the riders to scream.

"I don't know," said Val. "Can't you hear those people screaming?"

"That is the scream of fun," said Jeremy, but Val didn't look convinced.

(1) Why did Jeremy decide it was okay to wait a couple of hours to ride the Twisting Falls of Horror?

10 points

Jeremy decided it was okay to wait because the trip had _____
a week.

(2) Each person chose a ride to go on before Jeremy's choice of the Twisting Falls of Horror. Complete the chart to show which ride each person chose and why.

40 points

Ride Name	Reason
Spinning Swans	Val wanted to stay ①_____.
Ferris wheel	James ②_____.
③_____	Ling liked anything fast.
④_____	Jeremy's dad liked to drive.

2 Read the passage. Then answer the questions below using words from the passage.

10 points per question

The group watched as people exited the ride.

"How did everyone get wet?" asked Ling.

"The Falls of Horror are actually waterfalls that pass through caves," explained Jeremy. "Come on Val," he said to his sister who now looked even more unsure. "What can I do to convince you that this will be really fun?"

"Alright," she said, "but if I agree to ride the roller coaster, you have to rake the lawn for the rest of the fall."

Val was surprised when Jeremy didn't oppose her demand. She had thought it would work for sure, but now she was stuck riding the Twisting Falls of Horror.

Once she was sitting in her car, she stared up at the colossal first hill of the roller coaster. As the car inched up the hill, Val couldn't help smiling. She knew that the slow climb up the hill was what would give the car its speed for the rest of the ride. As the car raced down the track and traveled around a triple loop, she screamed with glee. By the time they traveled around the curve into the waterfall cave, she had decided to apologize to her brother. This was the best ride of the day, and she felt bad for having been so disagreeable before. She, Ling, and her father exited the ride soaking wet and laughing.

"That was awesome!" exclaimed Val, smiling at her brother and James. But when she saw Jeremy's pale face, her smile turned to a frown. "What's wrong, Jeremy?" she asked her brother.

"Nothing," he said, "I just didn't think it would be so scary."

(1) Why were the people exiting the roller coaster wet?

The people were wet because The Falls of Horror were _____

_____.

(2) What effect did the slow climb up the hill have on the car?

The slow climb up the hill was what would _____
for the rest of the ride.

(3) Why did Val decide to apologize to Jeremy?

Val decided to apologize to Jeremy because the ride he chose was the best ride of the day,

and she felt bad _____.

(4) Complete the chart below that shows the cause of each of Val's actions.   20 points

Cause	Effect
The car inched up the hill.	Val couldn't help smiling.
The car raced down the track.	Val ① _____.
Val saw ② _____.	Val's smile turned to a frown.

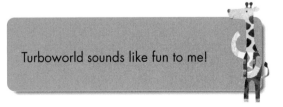

Turboworld sounds like fun to me!

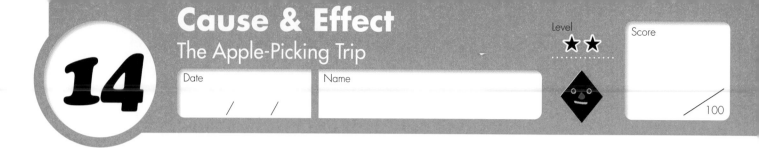

Cause & Effect
The Apple-Picking Trip

14

Date __/__/__

Name

Level ★★

Score /100

1 Read the passage. Then answer the questions below using words from the passage.

12 points per question

It was fall, and that meant the apples were ripe at the farm! Julie and her family were going to the Branner's farm outside of town to pick apples like they did every fall. This year, her father arranged for the family to get rides on the tractor, so everyone was especially excited. He usually forgot to make sure they had a seat on the tractor.

Julie thought the weather would be the same as it always was, and packed a sweater and a book for the car. Then she waited for the rest of her family to get ready. Her father was busy with work, and her mother was talking on the phone. When they realized that they were late, they all jumped into the car to leave.

"Honey, don't you think we should get some gas?" asked Julie's mother.

"No, I don't want to be late for the tractor," said her father as he drove quickly through the gray day. It started to rain, and Julie wished she had packed her raincoat.

They made it in time to get on the trailer behind the tractor. The rain was now coming down steadily, and it was cold, so Julie huddled in the corner of the trailer. She brought her knees up to her chest and shivered in the rain.

Then the tractor got stuck in a big mud puddle. The farm workers all got together and pushed, but the tractor wouldn't budge. It was stuck, all right. Now Julie and her parents had to get out and walk through the rain.

(1) Why was Julie's family especially excited this year?

Julie's family was especially excited because her father had _____

_____.

(2) Why did Julie not pack her raincoat?

Julie didn't pack her raincoat because she thought _____

_____.

(3) Why was the family late?

The family was late because her father was _____ and her mother

was _____.

(4) Why was Julie huddled in the corner of the trailer?

Julie was huddled in the corner of the trailer because the rain _____

_____, and _____.

(5) Why did Julie and her family have to walk through the rain?

Julie and her family had to walk through the rain because the _____

and wouldn't _____.

2 Read the passage below. Then answer the questions.

10 points per question

Julie tried to keep her spirits up, but she was cold and wet. They picked apples despite the rain, and Julie's mother even sang a little. After they filled their bags, though, they walked back to the car.

In the car, they put the heater on full blast and sunk into their seats. Julie had to huddle for a while again, grabbing her knees and trying to shake the shivers out of her body. Once the heater got going, she felt better. She watched the rain form rivers on the window. Then she noticed something flickering on and off in the front of the car.

"Dad, what's that light that keeps going on and off?" she asked.

"Oh no. That's the gas light, Julie," her father said and then got quiet.

They were still in farm country, and there wasn't a gas station in sight. The whole family sat with the radio off and hoped the gas would last.

It didn't. The car ran out of gas. Julie's father told them he would be right back and set off to find a gas station. Julie tried to sleep, but she was worried about her father and couldn't get comfortable. Finally, she arranged the apples just right and fell asleep on them.

When she woke up, she was in bed at home the next morning. She had a cold, too. It wasn't surprising that she had developed a cold after walking around in the cold rain without a coat. Despite her cold, she could smell something good cooking downstairs. Was that apple turnovers for breakfast? Maybe the apple-picking trip had not been so bad after all!

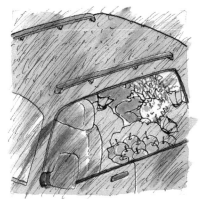

(1) Fill in the chart below using words from the passage.

Cause	Effect
Julie's father didn't get gas.	The car ① _____.
Julie didn't bring a raincoat to the apple-picking.	Julie ② _____.

(2) What word from the passage fits the following definition? Write the word below.

_____ = to draw the limbs in close to the body

(3) Why wasn't Julie surprised that she had developed a cold?

Julie was not surprised that she had developed a cold because she spent the day walking

_____ without a _____.

(4) Why did Julie think the apple-picking trip might not have been so bad after all?

Julie thought the apple-picking trip might not have been so bad because her mother was

making _____ for

_____.

Mmmm, that sounds good. I want apple pie!

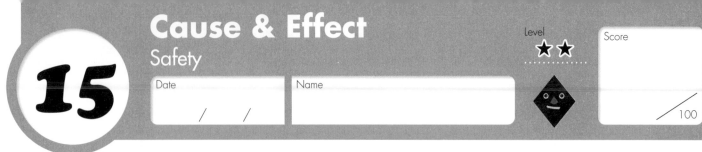

Cause & Effect
Safety

Level ★★

Date / /

Name

Score /100

15

1 Read the following passage. Complete the passage using the vocabulary words defined below.

5 points per question

Being safe is important. You can prevent injuries by taking (1)_____ like buckling your seat belt. Another precaution is knowing what (2)_____ to follow in the event of a fire. Taking precautions requires being aware of the (3)_____ in your environment. For example, an adult should (4)_____ when you use dangerous appliances.

Unfortunately, injuries are not always accidental. A (5)_____, such as angry words between two people, can lead to physical (6)_____. This should be avoided at all costs.

conflict	strong disagreement or struggle
procedure(s)	a method of doing something
hazard(s)	something that may cause damage or injury
violence	destructive action or force
precaution(s)	an action taken to prevent something bad from happening
supervise	to oversee an activity to make sure that it is done correctly

2 Read the passage. Then answer the questions below.

10 points per question

Safety, like any subject, can be learned. Knowing how to take precautions is one of the best ways to stay safe. Most accidents are caused by not taking simple precautions.

Hazards exist everywhere, even in unexpected places. Even such common activities as crossing a street, eating food, or playing sports can lead to accidents. Home, where people spend most of their time, is actually the most hazardous place.

Deciding to make safety a part of your life is a way to take responsibility for yourself. Safety rules and procedures are effective when people follow them properly.

(1) What causes most accidents?

Most accidents are caused by _____.

(2) What activities can lead to accidents?

_____ such as _____

_____ can lead to accidents.

(3) When are safety rules and procedures effective?

Safety rules and procedures are effective when _____.

Read the passage. Then answer the questions below.

Home should be the safest place of all, but carelessness makes it one of the most dangerous. Accidents can happen when people use tables and chairs as ladders and misuse kitchen appliances. Common hazards such as these cause the greatest number of injuries, including cuts, bruises, and sprains.

Many home accidents involve falls. Objects that are left on steps can cause others to trip over them. Every staircase should have a strong handrail and should be well lit. The kitchen is another place where many falls occur. Wiping up spilled water off the floor can prevent many accidents.

Burns occur mostly at home, and many of them happen in the kitchen. A hot stove is an obvious hazard that can cause painful burns. Cooking with heat should be done by adults, or at least with adult supervision.

House fires are also a serious problem. They often start unseen, so every house should have at least one smoke detector on each floor. These devices detect, or sense, any sign of smoke and warn you with an alarm.

Every family member should know what to do in case of a fire. Once agreed upon, these procedures should be reviewed and practiced together regularly. This practice will create a much safer home.

Accidents often occur in public places as well as at home. Accidents occur in these places for two main reasons. First, most visitors are unfamiliar with these places. Second, public places are often crowded. While you are in these places, pay attention to signs warning about any dangers.

(1) Why is the home one of the most dangerous places?

The home is one of the most dangerous places because of _____.

(2) What are some examples of common hazards that cause injuries?

Common hazards that cause injuries include using _____

_____ and misusing _____.

(3) Fill in the following chart about accidents in the home.

Cause	Effect
Objects _____	Falling on the stairs
_____ on the floor	Falling in the kitchen

(4) What are the two main reason accidents occur in public places?

Accidents occur in public places because visitors are

_____ and

_____.

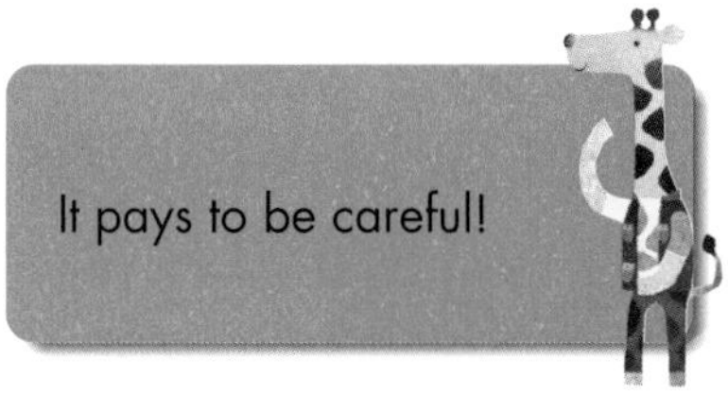

It pays to be careful!

Vocabulary Review

Date / /

Name

Score /100

1 Pick the correct word from the box to complete each sentence below.

5 points per question

convince	conflict	budge	precaution	demanded	develop

(1) The king _____ silence in the great hall.

(2) With the storm coming, we took the _____ of making sure we had flashlights.

(3) Julia had to work hard to _____ her mother to let her go to her friend's house.

(4) It is important to try to resolve a _____ before it gets out of hand.

(5) I kept pulling at my dog's leash, but he wouldn't _____.

(6) In some movies, it takes a long time for the story to _____.

2 Connect each word on the left to the correct definition on the right.

6 points per question

(1) hazard •

(2) huddle •

(3) procedure •

(4) violence •

(5) supervise •

• ⓐ a method of doing something

• ⓑ destructive action or force

• ⓒ to oversee an activity to make sure that it is done correctly

• ⓓ to draw the limbs in close to the body

• ⓔ something that may cause damage or injury

3 Complete the crossword puzzle using the sentences below as clues. Use capital letters.

5 points per question

Crossword grid with the following pre-filled letters:

(7) across top

(1) C . . . S . . . . (8)

(2) D . . . G . . . B

. . . . C

(6) . . G . K

(3) O . P . . . . (4) . V

. P . . . .

(5) X P . . . . . .

ACROSS

(1) The ice cream sundae at the local restaurant is not just big, it's ___?___.

(2) When my sister is hungry, she gets very ___?___.

(3) There was too much rain and the game was ___?___ until Saturday.

(4) Watch out for the ___?___ in the road ahead!

(5) Once the teacher ___?___ the problem, I understood it.

DOWN

(6) The tall boxer was ___?___ by a much shorter fighter, but it was a good match.

(7) We ___?___ the seating so that the cousins who were always fighting were at different tables.

(8) The porch lights ___?___ on and off in the rain.

If you struggle with a word, move on. When you come back to it, there might be more letters to use as hints!

Actions & Descriptions
Donald's First Camping Trip 1

17

Level ★★

Date   /   /

Name

Score   /100

1 Read the passage. Then answer the questions below.

15 points per question

Donald didn't want to admit it, but he was a little shy. He had short spiky brown hair, a round face, and was quiet. His mom never said anything, but she did suggest he sign up for the Little Scouts so he could meet more people. He agreed because he wanted to get out and hike.

After a couple months, he finally went on his first camping trip with the Little Scouts. They were only about an hour into their first hike of the day when Donald started to fall behind. Part of the problem was that there was so much wildlife to look at around the trail! Donald thought that animals in the wild were cool.

First, he saw a deer. It was beautiful. It was a young, brown deer with some white spots on its back, and a poofy little tail. The deer looked right at him, jumped a little, and ran away.

Then he saw a turtle walking slowly toward a stream next to the trail. It was a box turtle with a green circle and some brown squares in an interesting pattern on its back. Donald got down on all fours and talked to the little guy.

"How are you doing, turtle? Are you looking for something appetizing?" he asked the little animal.

Speaking of something that tasted good, Donald was hungry. He sat down and opened his bag. There, under his compass, was an energy bar. Break time!

(1) What did Donald look like?

Donald had _____ and _____.

(2) What did Donald finally do a couple months after signing up for the Little Scouts?

A couple months after signing up for the Little Scouts, Donald finally _____

_____.

Don't forget!

Stories have actions and descriptions. **Actions** are things that happen. **Descriptions** explain what something is or what something looks like.

Action   : *Donald went on his first camping trip.*
Description : *Donald had short spiky brown hair.*

---

(3) Write a **D** next to the statements below that are descriptions only.

( ) ⓐ Donald had short spiky brown hair.

( ) ⓑ A deer looked right at Donald.

( ) ⓒ The turtle had a green circle on its back.

2 Read the passage. Then answer the questions below.

Only when Donald finished his energy bar did he remember the rest of the troop.

"Oh no!" he shouted, and he jumped up. He put his backpack on and started to run up the trail. He shouted for his troop, but he didn't hear anything that sounded like other boys shouting back. The only sounds were the stream bubbling next to him and the birds in the trees.

He ran, and ran, and ran. He screamed and shouted frantically. Though he ran as fast and as far as he could, he couldn't catch up with his troop.

The sun started to set. There were orange streaks in the sky, and the birds were quiet. Donald didn't care about the wildlife any more. He was tired and sweaty and scared. When he almost couldn't walk any more, he found a tall boulder and scrambled to the top of the rock.

He shouted some more. No matter how frantically he waved or how loudly he shouted, he didn't see anyone else, and he didn't hear anything but his own voice. That was it. He was lost.

Now he had to try and remember his Little Scout training. He got out his compass and found north using the pointer. Why did north matter though? He didn't know where he was going, so knowing where north was was not going to help.

No, he had to find a place to camp that was near the path. That way, the troop leader or his buddy could find him. He thought he should probably also start a fire because it was getting cold.

(1) Write a **D** next to the statements below that are descriptions only.   35 points

( ) ⓐ Donald jumped up.

( ) ⓑ Donald shouted frantically.

( ) ⓒ There were orange streaks in the sky.

( ) ⓓ The birds were quiet.

( ) ⓔ Donald was sweaty and scared.

( ) ⓕ Donald scrambled to the top of a boulder.

( ) ⓖ Donald didn't hear anything but his own voice.

(2) What was the first thing Donald did after realizing that he was lost?   10 points

Donald got out _____
the pointer.

(3) What did Donald think he should do because it was getting cold?   10 points

Donald thought that because it was getting cold, he should

probably _____.

Do you like to hike?
Don't get lost!

Actions & Descriptions
Donald's First Camping Trip 2

18

Level
★★

Date   /   /

Name

Score

/100

1 Read the passage. Then answer the questions below.

Donald climbed down from the boulder and looked around the bottom of the huge rock. The path actually circled the rock, and there was a flat place with a little protection that was perfect. He sat down to think.

He didn't want to set up his tent. He still thought that the troop leader would come around the bend and find him at any moment. His buddy should have told the leader by now. They would be looking for him.

It was time to make the job easier for them by making a fire. Donald looked around the area for some tinder to make his fire. The best tinder was dried dead moss or small dry pieces of wood that had fallen from trees. Small dry leaves also worked because they would catch a spark and start a fire. He found lots of tinder around his boulder and stacked it up the way he had been taught. Then he gathered some bigger sticks and one small dry log to put on the fire once it started. He was ready to start the fire.

In order to get a spark, he had to strike his knife against the flint. His flint was a small gray stone he kept in a pouch. He struck it with his knife a few times and was happy to see a spark jump off the flint, catch in the tinder, and spread to make a small fire. Then he put the bigger sticks on the growing fire.

Eventually, he sat down and warmed his hands by the fire. It was exactly the kind of small fire Donald needed. He felt warmer already.

(1) Write a **D** next to the statements below that are description only.   35 points

(   ) ⓐ There was a flat place with a little protection that was a perfect place for Donald.

(   ) ⓑ Donald sat down to think.

(   ) ⓒ Donald started to gather tinder.

(   ) ⓓ The best tinder was dried dead moss or leaves.

(   ) ⓔ He found some bigger sticks and a dry log.

(   ) ⓕ Donald made a spark with his flint.

(   ) ⓖ It was exactly the kind of small fire Donald needed.

(2) Number Donald's actions in the order they appear in the story.   20 points

(   ) ⓐ Donald found tinder.

(   ) ⓑ Donald found a good place to make a fire.

(   ) ⓒ Donald struck his flint to get a spark.

(   ) ⓓ Donald warmed his hands by the fire.

(   ) ⓔ Donald put bigger sticks on the growing fire.

Read the passage. Then fill in the chart below using words from the passage.

9 points per question

With the fire going, Donald felt a little better. He warmed his fingers and his toes by the fire and wished he had some marshmallows to put in the fire. He was sure his troop was eating them now. He was hungry, too. He tore open another energy bar and ate it quickly. It was not quite the same as a marshmallow.

Donald huddled by the fire. He was still a little scared. He was lost in the wilderness, and there wasn't much he could do. There was no gas station where he could ask directions and no phone to use. There was wildlife all around him, too.

Donald thought he might as well put his tent up if they weren't going to find him that night. The tent was complicated, though. He struggled with the poles and almost put one in the fire by accident.

He was about to give up when he heard a racket out beyond his fire. The noise was loud, but he couldn't figure out what it was. Who was making that racket? He hoped it wasn't a bear coming down the path.

He listened for the noise again. The next time it was louder, and he knew what it was. It was his name! He picked up a log from the ground and waved it in the air and yelled and yelled.

Finally, his troop leader and buddy came around the bend. Donald was so happy to see them that he hugged them both. The leader was a little angry, but he said Donald did the right thing by staying near the path with a fire. His buddy apologized for losing him, but Donald was too happy to care.

Descriptions of Donald and his surroundings	Donald's actions
He was hungry.	He tore (1)_____ _____ and _____.
He was still a little scared.	He (2)_____ by _____.
The tent was complicated.	He (3)_____ with _____.
The noise was loud.	He heard a (4)_____ _____.
He was (5)_____ his buddy and troop leader.	He hugged them both.

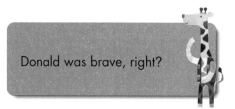

Donald was brave, right?

© Kumon Publishing Co., Ltd. 37

Actions & Descriptions
Sonya and Tanya 1

Level ★★

Date / /

Name

Score /100

19

1 Read the passage. Then answer the questions below.

Sonya and Tanya were twins, and they were very competitive. Every year, they played the same sport and each worked hard to be better than the other. Their closets were filled with board games that they had played against each other for ages. Any time they could, they tried to make a game out of what they were doing.

One day they got their seeds for a project in science class. No one was surprised that they once again created a competition out of almost nothing. The science project was an experiment on how plants grow. Each student was supposed to cultivate two seeds in different conditions and then compare the results. They would water and store one seed in the light and one seed in the dark. Then they would record the height every day. At the end, they were going to graph the height of each plant to see how light affected their growth.

"My plants are going to grow taller than yours," Tanya said on the ride home from school.

"You are dreaming!" exclaimed Sonya quickly. "Your seeds have no chance."

The way that Sonya replied with such energy annoyed Tanya, and they spent the rest of the ride home in silence. The fact that they were silent did not bother their mother, who was getting tired of their constant fighting. Their mother turned up the volume on the radio and hummed along to a song she liked. Her twins looked out of separate windows quietly.

(1) Fill in the chart below using words from the passage.

5 points per question

Descriptions	Actions
The twins were very competitive.	Every year, they ①_____ _____ and each ②_____ _____.
The science project was an experiment on how plants grow.	Each student was supposed to cultivate ③_____ _____ and ④_____.

(2) Write a **D** next to the statements below that are descriptions only.

20 points for completion

( ) ⓐ Tanya said that her plants would grow taller than Sonya's.

( ) ⓑ The twins were quiet.

( ) ⓒ Their mother turned up the volume on the radio.

( ) ⓓ Their mother was not bothered by their silence.

© Kumon Publishing Co., Ltd.

2 Read the passage and complete the chart below.

When they got home, they raced to their rooms to set up their seeds because they were excited about the competition. They each cleaned off their window sills for the seeds that were supposed to be grown in the light. Both girls found a little room in the closet for the seeds that were supposed to stay in the dark. They both went down to the kitchen for water at the same time, too.

"Are you ready to lose?" asked Sonya playfully.

"Only if losing means I have the tallest plant," replied Tanya.

"You girls are ridiculous!" exclaimed their mother who was boiling water for her tea. "It's so silly to compete like this on everything!"

The girls ran back upstairs to tend to their plants. Each girl had different ideas about how to make their plants grow, and their personalities came through in the way they cultivated their seeds.

Sonya was the talkative twin. She liked to entertain people by talking, singing, and dancing, so she took her seed from the window sill and talked to it. She danced around the room with it. She sang to it, too. The seed was treated to all of Sonya's favorite songs.

Tanya was quieter than her sister. She liked to write stories, but she knew her seed couldn't read. So Tanya wrote a story about growing big and tall, and then she whispered the story to her plant all afternoon.

Descriptions	Actions
Both Sisters The sisters were (1)_____ about the competition.	They (2)_____ to set up their seeds.
Sonya Sonya was the (3)_____. She liked to entertain people by (4)_____ _____.	She took her seed from the window sill and (5)_____. She (6)_____ _____ and sang to it.
Tanya Tanya was (7)_____ _____. She liked to (8)_____.	Tanya (9)_____ _____, and then she (10)_____ _____ all afternoon.

Who do you think will grow the tallest plant?

20

Actions & Descriptions
Sonya and Tanya 2

Level ★★

Date / /

Name

Score /100

1 Read the passage. Then answer the questions below.

Over the next couple of days, the girls spent almost all of their time in their rooms with their seeds. They were very friendly girls to begin with. Now it seemed that they had made a pair of new friends, and they did many activities together with their new friends — the seeds. Sonya listened to the radio with her seed, and Tanya read her book out loud to her seed.

Sonya wanted her seed to grow faster. After two days, she saw only the very top of a sprout coming through her soil. She found her mother to complain.

"Mom, why won't my seed grow faster?" she asked.

"There you go being ridiculous again! You have to be patient if you want to be a good gardener," her mother said. "It will take some time before your plant grows tall."

Sonya was not a very patient girl. She didn't like waiting for anything, so Sonya groaned at her mother and ran back up to her room. There, she turned the music up louder and turned the lights on even though it was daytime.

A little while later Tanya came downstairs.

"Mom, what can I do to make my seed grow faster than Sonya's?" asked Tanya.

"Oh, you are just like your sister! I'm not going to help you two on this one," laughed her mother.

Tanya groaned and ran upstairs like her sister. She was also not a patient girl. She read her journal to her plant again, but she read it louder. She asked her plant questions even though she knew there would be no response.

(1) Fill out the chart below.

10 points per question

Descriptions	Actions
They were ①_____ _____.	They made a pair of new friends, and they did many activities together with their new friends, the seeds.
Sonya was not a very patient girl.	Sonya ②_____ and ③_____.

(2) What did Tanya do right after her mother told her she wouldn't help?   10 points

Tanya _____.

2 Read the passage and answer the questions below.

A couple of days later, the house awoke to a scream. Sonya was shouting in her room when the whole family came in. She was very upset.

"What's wrong, Sonya?" asked her mother.

"Where's my seed?!" exclaimed Sonya.

There, on her window sill, was an empty cup and some dirt. There was no seed, however.

"Did you take my seed?!" Sonya asked her sister.

"No, I didn't take your seed," shouted Tanya back.

"Hold on girls, slow down. Look here on your floor, I think there's some evidence in this case," said their mother.

Indeed, the evidence was strong. There was a little set of dirty paw prints leading away from the window sill. It looked like their cat Whiskers did it.

"Oh no, Whiskers ate my plant!" said Sonya and started crying.

Tanya felt very bad for her sister. She didn't know what to do, but she didn't care about growing a taller seed than her sister any more.

"Don't cry, Sonya," said Tanya, "we'll just explain what happened. You can help me take care of my plant, and we'll turn in one project."

"Really?" said Sonya through red eyes. "You would do that for me?" she asked.

"Of course! You're my sister!" said Tanya, and they hugged.

Now their mother was crying.

"It's so nice to see you on the same team! Usually you are opposed to doing anything together. I'm so proud you're working together," said their mother as she hugged her two twins tightly.

(1) Write a **D** next to the statements below that are descriptions only.   40 points

(   ) ⓐ The family awoke to a scream.

(   ) ⓑ Sonya was very upset.

(   ) ⓒ On her window sill was an empty cup and some dirt.

(   ) ⓓ There were some dirty paw prints leading away from the window.

(   ) ⓔ Sonya cried.

(   ) ⓕ Sonya had red eyes.

(   ) ⓖ Tanya offered to help.

(   ) ⓗ Their mother hugged them tightly.

(2) Why was their mother crying?   20 points

Their mother was crying because it was nice to see them _____

and she was so _____ they were _____.

Working together is a great idea!

Vocabulary Review

Level ★★

Date / /

Name

Score /100

1 Pick the correct word from the box to complete each sentence below.

6 points per question

opposed	boulder	wildlife	compass	eventually

(1) The _____ around my grandfather's house in Africa is amazing.

(2) "You'll speak _____," my sister said when I gave her the silent treatment.

(3) The local team was _____ by a much stronger team from the city.

(4) The hawk landed on a nearby _____ and looked down on the scouts.

(5) I used my _____ to find the trail again.

2 Connect each word on the left to the correct definition on the right.

5 points per question

(1) journal •   • ⓐ to help something grow

(2) flint •   • ⓑ to shout or cry out

(3) cultivate •   • ⓒ deserving to be laughed at, or considered silly or absurd

(4) appetizing •   • ⓓ a record of daily activities or experiences

(5) ridiculous •   • ⓔ a material used for making a spark

(6) exclaimed •   • ⓕ pleasing to the taste

3 Complete the crossword puzzle using the sentences below as clues. Use capital letters.

5 points per question

ACROSS

(1) When my brother put on his clown costume, he looked ___?___.

(2) You have to be ___?___ when training a dog. They don't learn right away!

(3) "The ice cream truck is on our corner!" ___?___ my little brother.

(4) Knowing how to find water is a key to surviving in the ___?___.

DOWN

(5) Gathering ___?___ is the first step to making a fire.

(6) The dogs barking out in the yard made quite a ___?___.

(7) After a season of hard work, she was able to ___?___ a blooming rose bush.

(8) I write in my ___?___ every night before bed.

Remember to check the previous pages for hints, too!

Characters
Alice's Adventures in Wonderland 1

Level ★★

Date / /

Name

Score /100

1 Read the passage from *Alice's Adventures in Wonderland* by Lewis Carroll. Then answer the questions below using words from the passage.

10 points per question

> CHAPTER I. Down the Rabbit-Hole
>
> Alice was beginning to get very tired of sitting by her sister on the bank, and of having nothing to do: once or twice she had peeped into the book her sister was reading, but it had no pictures or conversations in it, 'and what is the use of a book,' thought Alice 'without pictures or conversation?'
>
> So she was considering in her own mind (as well as she could, for the hot day made her feel very sleepy and stupid), whether the pleasure of making a daisy-chain would be worth the trouble of getting up and picking the daisies, when suddenly a White Rabbit with pink eyes ran close by her.
>
> There was nothing so *very* remarkable in that; nor did Alice think it so *very* much out of the way to hear the Rabbit say to itself, 'Oh dear! Oh dear! I shall be late!' (when she thought it over afterwards, it occurred to her that she ought to have wondered at this, but at the time it all seemed quite natural); but when the Rabbit actually *took a watch out of its waistcoat-pocket*, and looked at it, and then hurried on, Alice started to her feet, for it flashed across her mind that she had never before seen a rabbit with either a waistcoat-pocket, or a watch to take out of it, and burning with curiosity, she ran across the field after it, and fortunately was just in time to see it pop down a large rabbit-hole under the hedge.
>
> In another moment down went Alice after it, never once considering how in the world she was to get out again.

(1) How was Alice feeling about what she was doing?

Alice was beginning to get _____

_____ , and of _____ .

(2) How did the hot day make Alice feel?

The hot day made Alice feel _____ .

(3) Who ran by Alice as she was thinking of making a daisy-chain?

_____ with _____ ran by her as she was thinking of making a daisy-chain.

(4) What action by the rabbit caused Alice to run after it?

The rabbit took _____ ,
and looked at it, and hurried on.

2 Read this passage, which picks up the story at a later scene. Then answer the questions below using words from the passage.

12 points per question

… 'What a curious feeling!' said Alice; 'I must be shutting up like a telescope.'

And so it was indeed: she was now only ten inches high, and her face brightened up at the thought that she was now the right size for going through the little door into that lovely garden. First, however, she waited for a few minutes to see if she was going to shrink any further: she felt a little nervous about this; 'for it might end, you know,' said Alice to herself, 'in my going out altogether, like a candle. I wonder what I should be like then?' And she tried to fancy what the flame of a candle is like after the candle is blown out, for she could not remember ever having seen such a thing.

After a while, finding that nothing more happened, she decided on going into the garden at once; but, alas for poor Alice! when she got to the door, she found she had forgotten the little golden key, and when she went back to the table for it, she found she could not possibly reach it: she could see it quite plainly through the glass, and she tried her best to climb up one of the legs of the table, but it was too slippery; and when she had tired herself out with trying, the poor little thing sat down and cried.

'Come, there's no use in crying like that!' said Alice to herself, rather sharply; 'I advise you to leave off this minute!'

(1) What did Alice look like now?

Alice was now only _____.

(2) Why did she wait a few minutes before going through the door?

Alice waited a few minutes in order to see _____

_____.

(3) Why couldn't Alice get into the garden?

Alice couldn't get into the garden because she had forgotten _____

_____, and when she went back to the table for it, she found _____

_____.

(4) How did Alice react when she couldn't get to the key?

When she couldn't get to the key, Alice _____.

(5) How did Alice react after she started crying?

Alice told herself, rather _____,

to stop _____.

Can you imagine being ten inches high?

23

Characters
Alice's Adventures in Wonderland 2

Level ★★

Date / /

Name

Score /100

1 Read the passage. Then answer the questions below using words from the passage.

She generally gave herself very good advice, (though she very seldom followed it), and sometimes she scolded herself so severely as to bring tears into her eyes; and once she remembered trying to box her own ears for having cheated herself in a game of croquet she was playing against herself, for this curious child was very fond of pretending to be two people. 'But it's no use now,' thought poor Alice, 'to pretend to be two people! Why, there's hardly enough of me left to make *one* respectable person!'

Soon her eye fell on a little glass box that was lying under the table: she opened it, and found in it a very small cake, on which the words 'EAT ME' were beautifully marked in currants. 'Well, I'll eat it,' said Alice, 'and if it makes me grow larger, I can reach the key; and if it makes me grow smaller, I can creep under the door; so either way I'll get into the garden, and I don't care which happens!'

She ate a little bit, and said anxiously to herself, 'Which way? Which way?', holding her hand on the top of her head to feel which way it was growing, and she was quite surprised to find that she remained the same size: to be sure, this generally happens when one eats cake, but Alice had got so much into the way of expecting nothing but out-of-the-way things to happen, that it seemed quite dull and stupid for life to go on in the common way.

So she set to work, and very soon finished off the cake.

(1) Fill in the chart below about Alice's descriptions and actions. 15 points per question

Descriptions of Alice	Actions by Alice
Alice generally gave herself ①_____.	Sometimes Alice scolded herself so severely as to bring tears into her eyes.
Alice was fond of pretending to be two people.	One time, she tried to box her own ears for ②_____ _____ of croquet she was playing against herself.

(2) What was Alice surprised about after eating a little bit of the cake? 10 points

Alice was surprised to find that _____ after eating the cake.

(3) Why did Alice think she was going to change size after eating a little bit of the cake? 10 points

Alice thought she would change size because she had got so much into the way of

_____ but out-of-the-way things to happen, that it seemed quite

_____.

2 Read the passage, which picks up Alice's story a little while later. Then answer the questions below using words from the passage.

10 points per question

... Just then her head struck against the roof of the hall: in fact she was now more than nine feet high, and she at once took up the little golden key and hurried off to the garden door.

Poor Alice! It was as much as she could do, lying down on one side, to look through into the garden with one eye; but to get through was more hopeless than ever: she sat down and began to cry again.

'You ought to be ashamed of yourself,' said Alice, 'a great girl like you,' (she might well say this), 'to go on crying in this way! Stop this moment, I tell you!' But she went on all the same, shedding gallons of tears, until there was a large pool all round her, about four inches deep and reaching half down the hall.

After a time she heard a little pattering of feet in the distance, and she hastily dried her eyes to see what was coming. It was the White Rabbit returning, splendidly dressed, with a pair of white kid gloves in one hand and a large fan in the other: he came trotting along in a great hurry, muttering to himself as he came, 'Oh! the Duchess, the Duchess! Oh! won't she be savage if I've kept her waiting!' Alice felt so desperate that she was ready to ask help of any one; so, when the Rabbit came near her, she began, in a low, timid voice, 'If you please, sir — '

(1) How tall was Alice now?

Alice was now _____.

(2) Why did Alice start to cry again?

Alice started to cry because getting through the door was _____

_____.

(3) What did Alice tell herself after she started crying?

After she started crying, Alice told herself she _____

_____ to go on crying in that way.

(4) How was the White Rabbit dressed this time?

The White Rabbit was _____, with a _____

_____ and a _____.

(5) How was the White Rabbit acting this time?

The White Rabbit came _____, muttering

_____ as he came.

What an interesting rabbit!

Characters
Alice's Adventures in Wonderland 3

24

Level
★★★

Score

/ 100

Date / /

Name

1 Read the passage. Then answer the questions below using words from the passage.

10 points per question

> The Rabbit started violently, dropped the white kid gloves and the fan, and scurried away into the darkness as hard as he could go.
>
> Alice took up the fan and gloves, and, as the hall was very hot, she kept fanning herself all the time she went on talking: 'Dear, dear! How queer everything is to-day! And yesterday things went on just as usual. I wonder if I've been changed in the night? Let me think: was I the same when I got up this morning? I almost think I can remember feeling a little different. But if I'm not the same, the next question is, Who in the world am I? Ah, *that's* the great puzzle!' And she began thinking over all the children she knew that were of the same age as herself, to see if she could have been changed for any of them.
>
> 'I'm sure I'm not Ada,' she said, 'for her hair goes in such long ringlets, and mine doesn't go in ringlets at all; and I'm sure I can't be Mabel, for I know all sorts of things, and she, oh! she knows such a very little! Besides, *she's* she, and I'm I, and — oh dear, how puzzling it all is! I'll try if I know all the things I used to know. Let me see: four times five is twelve, and four times six is thirteen, and four times seven is — oh dear!

(1) How did the White Rabbit respond to Alice's request?

The Rabbit _____, dropped _____

_____, and _____ into the darkness as hard as

he could go.

(2) What did Alice wonder about herself after the Rabbit left?

Alice wondered if she had been _____.

(3) What was the great puzzle for Alice?

The great puzzle for Alice was if she was _____ any more, then

who _____ was she?

(4) Fill in the chart below using words from the passage.

15 points per question

Alice's Friends	Descriptions of Alice's Friends
Ada	She has hair that ①_____ _____.
②_____	She knows very little.

2 Read the passage, which picks up Alice's story when she meets the Queen. Then answer the questions below using words from the story.

10 points per question

... CHAPTER VIII. The Queen's Croquet-Ground

A large rose-tree stood near the entrance of the garden: the roses growing on it were white, but there were three gardeners at it, busily painting them red. Alice thought this a very curious thing, and she went nearer to watch them, and just as she came up to them she heard one of them say, 'Look out now, Five! Don't go splashing paint over me like that!'

'I couldn't help it,' said Five, in a sulky tone; 'Seven jogged my elbow.'

On which Seven looked up and said, 'That's right, Five! Always lay the blame on others!'

'You'd better not talk!' said Five. 'I heard the Queen say only yesterday you deserved to be beheaded!'

'What for?' said the one who had spoken first.

'That's none of *your* business, Two!' said Seven.

'Yes, it *is* his business!' said Five, 'and I'll tell him — it was for bringing the cook tulip-roots instead of onions.'

Seven flung down his brush, and had just begun 'Well, of all the unjust things — ' when his eye chanced to fall upon Alice, as she stood watching them, and he checked himself suddenly: the others looked round also, and all of them bowed low.

'Would you tell me,' said Alice, a little timidly, 'why you are painting those roses?'

Five and Seven said nothing, but looked at Two. Two began in a low voice, 'Why the fact is, you see, Miss, this here ought to have been a *red* rose-tree, and we put a white one in by mistake; and if the Queen was to find it out, we should all have our heads cut off, you know.

(1) What were the gardeners doing to the rose-tree?

The gardeners were _____ the roses _____.

(2) Why was one of the gardeners mad at Five?

One of the gardeners was mad at Five because he had been _____

_____ him.

(3) Why did the Queen say that Seven deserved to be beheaded?

The Queen said that Seven deserved to be beheaded because he brought the _____

_____.

(4) Why were the gardeners painting the rose-tree?

The gardeners were painting the rose-tree red

because they put a _____

_____.

The gardeners don't seem to be good at their job, do they?

Characters

Alice's Adventures in Wonderland 4

25

Level ★★★

Score

Date / /

Name

/100

1 Read the passage. Then fill in the chart below using words from the passage.

5 points per question

'So you see, Miss, we're doing our best, afore she comes, to — ' At this moment Five, who had been anxiously looking across the garden, called out 'The Queen! The Queen!' and the three gardeners instantly threw themselves flat upon their faces. There was a sound of many footsteps, and Alice looked round, eager to see the Queen.

First came ten soldiers carrying clubs; these were all shaped like the three gardeners, oblong and flat, with their hands and feet at the corners: next the ten courtiers*; these were ornamented all over with diamonds, and walked two and two, as the soldiers did. After these came the royal children; there were ten of them, and the little dears came jumping merrily along hand in hand, in couples: they were all ornamented with hearts. Next came the guests, mostly Kings and Queens, and among them Alice recognised the White Rabbit: it was talking in a hurried nervous manner, smiling at everything that was said, and went by without noticing her. Then followed the Knave of Hearts, carrying the King's crown on a crimson velvet cushion; and, last of all this grand procession, came *the King and Queen of Hearts*.

*courtier – a member of the royal court

Character(s) in the Procession	Description of the Character(s)
Ten soldiers	These came (1)_____ clubs and were shaped like (2)_____.
Ten courtiers	These were (3)_____ with diamonds, and walked two by two.
The royal children	There were ten of them. They came (4)_____ _____, in couples and were ornamented with hearts.
The (5)_____	These were mostly Kings and Queens, but also included was the White Rabbit.
The Knave of Hearts	He carried (6)_____ on (7)_____.
The (8)_____ _____	They were last in the procession.

© Kumon Publishing Co., Ltd.

Read the passage. Then answer the questions below using words from the passage.

12 points per question

Alice was rather doubtful whether she ought not to lie down on her face like the three gardeners, but she could not remember ever having heard of such a rule at processions; 'and besides, what would be the use of a procession,' thought she, 'if people had all to lie down upon their faces, so that they couldn't see it?' So she stood still where she was, and waited.

When the procession came opposite to Alice, they all stopped and looked at her, and the Queen said severely 'Who is this?' She said it to the Knave of Hearts, who only bowed and smiled in reply.

'Idiot!' said the Queen, tossing her head impatiently; and, turning to Alice, she went on, 'What's your name, child?'

'My name is Alice, so please your Majesty,' said Alice very politely; but she added, to herself, 'Why, they're only a pack of cards, after all. I needn't be afraid of them!'

'And who are *these*?' said the Queen, pointing to the three gardeners who were lying round the rose-tree; for, you see, as they were lying on their faces, and the pattern on their backs was the same as the rest of the pack, she could not tell whether they were gardeners, or soldiers, or courtiers, or three of her own children.

'How should I know?' said Alice, surprised at her own courage. 'It's no business of *mine*.'

The Queen turned crimson with fury, and, after glaring at her for a moment like a wild beast, screamed 'Off with her head! Off — '

'Nonsense!' said Alice, very loudly and decidedly, and the Queen was silent.

(1) What were Alice's reasons for being doubtful about lying down on her face?

She could not _____

_____ processions, and she also wondered what the use of a procession

would be, if people had _____

_____, so _____ at all.

(2) How did Alice reply to the Queen's first question?

Alice replied _____ with her name.

(3) Why couldn't the Queen tell who was lying face down on the ground?

The Queen couldn't tell who was lying face down because the pattern _____

_____.

(4) How did Alice reply to the Queen's second question?

Alice replied, surprised at her own _____, that it was _____
of hers.

(5) How did Alice reply to the Queen's order?

Alice replied, very _____,

that it was _____.

Alice is so brave!

Vocabulary Review

Date   /   /

Name

Score

/100

1 Pick the correct word from the box to complete each sentence below.

6 points per question

courtiers	script	represent	waistcoat	convert	resources

(1) My grandfather keeps a watch in his _____ pocket.

(2) Jill had to memorize all the lines in her _____ before the play started.

(3) The _____ all agreed that the king should act quickly.

(4) It takes all sorts of _____ to build a skyscraper.

(5) The stars on the American flag _____ all 50 states in the country.

(6) Plants _____ nutrients in the soil into energy so that they can grow.

2 Read the sentences below. Then circle the word that is the closest in meaning to the underlined word in the sentence.

6 points per question

(1) We saw a bunny in our backyard, but he rapidly went down a hole.

    slowly   quickly   angrily

(2) The entire affair with the talking playing cards was puzzling to Alice.

    confusing   interesting   upsetting

(3) The procession was incredibly exciting. The clowns came first, and then the dancers.

    party   march   show

(4) My favorite skirt is ornamented with fake rubies and diamonds.

    covered   filled   decorated

Complete the crossword puzzle using the sentences below as clues. Use capital letters.

5 points per question

[Crossword grid with pre-filled letters: (5) R, (1) T, C, (6) C, R, (7), (8), (2) E, T, C, L, S, G, E, K, (3) X, C, N, D, (4) E, D]

ACROSS

(1) The captain extended his ___?___ to see if the ship was approaching land.

(2) Our drama teacher is very ___?___ and always seems like she's acting.

(3) James was ___?___ to have a really enjoyable time at the waterpark that weekend.

(4) Our dog is always ___?___ hair all over the place.

DOWN

(5) Mother said I should put on a ___?___ shirt because the restaurant was nice.

(6) There is something very ___?___ about a rabbit that has a clock.

(7) ___?___, there are five people in my family: my parents, my brother, my sister, and me.

(8) The queen was ___?___ dressed in her full gown and crown.

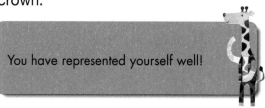

You have represented yourself well!

27

Date   /   /

Name

Score
/100

---

1 Read the passage from *My Side of the Mountain* by Jean Craighead George about a boy and his falcon, Frightful. Then answer the questions below using words from the passage.

8 points per question

IN WHICH   I Learn About Birds and People

Frightful and I settled down to living in snow. We went to bed early, slept late, ate the mountain harvest, and explored the country alone. Oh, the deer walked with us, the foxes followed in our footsteps, the winter birds flew over our heads, but mostly we were alone in the white wilderness. It was nice. It was very, very nice. My deerskin rabbit-lined suit was so warm that even when my breath froze in my nostrils, my body was snug and comfortable. Frightful fluffed on the coldest days, but a good flight into the air around the mountain would warm her, and she would come back to my fist with a thump and a flip. This was her signal of good spirits.

I did not become lonely. Many times during the summer I had thought of the "long winter months ahead" with some fear. I had read so much about the loneliness of the farmer, the trapper, the woodsman during the bleakness of winter that I had come to believe it. The winter was as exciting as the summer — maybe more so. The birds were magnificent and almost tame. They talked to each other, warned each other, fought for food, for kingship, and for the right to make the most noise. Sometimes I would sit in my doorway, which became an entrance to behold — a portico* of pure white snow, adorned with snowmen — and watch them with endless interest.

---

*portico – a porch or walkway with a roof supported by columns

(1) What did the boy do to settle down to living in snow?

He went _____, slept _____, and ate the _____.

(2) How did the boy describe living alone in the white wilderness?

_____.

(3) How warm was the boy's deerskin rabbit-lined suit?

It was so warm that even when his _____,

his _____.

(4) What was Frightful's signal of good spirits?

To signal her good spirits, Frightful would _____ to the boy's _____

_____.

(5) Why had the boy thought of the "long winter months ahead" with some fear?

He was afraid because he had _____

of the _____, and _____

during the _____ that he had _____

_____.

From MY SIDE OF THE MOUNTAIN by Jean Craighead George, copyright © 1959, renewed © 1987 by Jean Craighead George. Used by permission of Dutton Children's Books, A Division of Penguin Young Readers Group, A Member of Penguin Group (USA) Inc. 345 Hudson Street, New York, NY 10014. All rights reserved.

They reminded me of Third Avenue, and I gave them the names that seemed to fit.

There was Mr. Bracket. He lived on the first floor of our apartment house, and no one could sit on his step or even make a noise near his door without being chased. Mr. Bracket, the chickadee, spent most of his time chasing the young chickadees through the woods. Only his mate could share his favorite perches and feeding places.

Then there were Mrs. O'Brien, Mrs. Callaway, and Mrs. Federio. On Third Avenue they would all go off to the market together first thing in the morning, talking and pushing and stopping to lecture to children in gutters and streets. Mrs. Federio always followed Mrs. O'Brien, and Mrs. O'Brien always followed Mrs. Callaway in talking and pushing and even in buying an apple. And there they were again in my hemlock; three busy chickadees. They would flit and rush around and click and fly from one eating spot to another. They were noisy, scolding and busily following each other. All the other chickadees followed them, and they made way only for Mr. Bracket.

The chickadees, like the people on Third Avenue, had their favorite routes to and from the best food supplies. They each had their own resting perches and each had a little shelter in a tree cavity to which they would fly when the day was over.

*hemlock – a type of evergreen tree

(1) What did Mr. Bracket the chickadee do?

Mr. Bracket the chickadee spent most of his time _____

_____ .

(2) What were the chickadees named Mrs. O'Brien, Mrs. Callaway, and Mrs. Federio like?

The three busy chickadees were _____ and _____

_____ .

(3) Fill in the chart below.

Actions of the three ladies
Mrs. Federio always ①_____, who always ②_____.

Actions of the three chickadees
They would ③_____ around and ④_____ _____ to another.

These are some interesting chickadees!

Reading Comprehension
My Side of the Mountain 2

28

Level ★★★

Score

Date   /   /

Name

/100

1 Read the passage. Then answer the questions below using words from the passage.

10 points per question

They would chatter and call good night and make a big fuss before they parted; and then the forest would be as quiet as the apartment house on Third Avenue when all the kids were off the streets and all the parents had said their last words to each other and everyone had gone to their own little hole.

Sometimes when the wind howled and the snows blew, the chickadees would be out for only a few hours. Even Mr. Bracket, who had been elected by the chickadees to test whether or not it was too stormy for good hunting, would appear for a few hours and disappear. Sometimes I would find him just sitting quietly on a limb next to the bole* of a tree, all fluffed up and doing nothing. There was no one who more enjoyed doing nothing on a bad day than Mr. Bracket of Third Avenue.

Frightful, the two Mr. Brackets, and I shared this feeling. When the ice and sleet and snow drove down through the hemlocks, we all holed up.

I looked at my calendar pole one day, and realized that it was almost Christmas. Bando will come, I thought. I'll have to prepare a feast and make a present for him. I took stock of the frozen venison* and decided that there were enough steaks for us to eat nothing but venison for a month. I scooped under the snow for teaberry plants to boil down and pour over snowballs for dessert.

bole – trunk / *venison* – meat, usually deer meat

(1) What was the forest like at night?

At night, the forest would be as _____

_____ when all the kids _____ and all the

parents _____ other.

(2) What would the chickadees do when the wind howled and the snows blew?

They would be out _____. Mr. Bracket would test _____

_____, appear for a

few hours, and _____.

(3) How did Mr. Bracket of Third Avenue feel about a "bad day"?

There was no one _____

_____.

(4) What did Frightful, the two Mr. Brackets, and the boy do on a bad day?

When the ice and _____, through the hemlocks,

they _____.

2 Read the passage that picks up the story once Professor Bando arrives. Then answer the questions below.

15 points per question

… "And now, I have something to show you," he said. He reached in his coat pocket and took out a newspaper clipping. It was from a New York paper, and it read:

WILD BOY SUSPECTED LIVING OFF DEER AND NUTS IN WILDERNESS OF CATSKILLS

I looked at Bando and leaned over to read the headline myself.

"Have you been talking?" I asked.

"Me? Don't be ridiculous. You have had several visitors other than me."

"The fire warden — the old lady!" I cried out.

"Now, Thoreau, this could only be a rumor. Just because it is in print, doesn't mean it's true. Before you get excited, sit still and listen." He read: " 'Residents of Delhi, in the Catskill Mountains, report that a wild boy, who lives off deer and nuts, is hiding out in the mountains. " 'Several hunters stated that this boy stole deer from them during hunting season.' "

"I did not!" I shouted. "I only took the ones they had wounded and couldn't find."

"Well, that's what they told their wives when they came home without their deer. Anyway, listen to this: " 'This wild boy has been seen from time to time by Catskill residents, some of whom believe he is crazy!' "

"Well, that's a terrible thing to say!"

"Just awful," he stated. "Any normal red-blooded American boy wants to live in a tree house and trap his own food. They just don't do it, that's all." "Read on," I said.

(1) How did the headline in the newspaper describe the "wild boy"?

The headline suggested that the boy was wild because he was _____

_____ in the _____ of the Catskill Mountains.

(2) Which deer did the boy take from the hunters?

The boy took deer that the hunters had _____.

(3) Why did Bando suggest that the hunters accused the boy of stealing their deer?

Bando suggested that they needed something to tell _____ when

they _____.

(4) Why didn't Bando agree with the Catskill residents?

Bando disagreed because he thought any normal _____

_____ wanted _____

_____. The only difference was that those boys just didn't _____.

Would you like to live in a tree house?

Reading Comprehension

My Side of the Mountain 3

Level ★★★

Score

Date / /

Name

/100

29

1 Read the passage. Then answer the questions below using words from the passage.

15 points per question

" 'Officials say that there is no evidence of any boy living alone in the mountains and add that all abandoned houses and sheds are routinely checked for just such events. Nevertheless, the residents are sure that such a boy exists!' End story."

"That's a lot of nonsense!" I leaned back against the bedstead and smiled.

"Ho, ho, don't think that ends it," Bando said, and reached in his pocket for another clipping. "This one is dated December fifth, the other was November twenty-third. Shall I read?"

"Yes."

OLD WOMAN REPORTS MEETING WILD BOY WHILE PICKING STRAWBERRIES IN CATSKILLS

" 'Mrs. Thomas Fielder, ninety-seven, resident of Delhi, N.Y., told this reporter that she met a wild boy on Bitter Mountain last June while gathering her annual strawberry jelly supply.

" 'She said the boy was brown-haired, dusty, and wandering aimlessly around the mountains. However, she added, he seemed to be in good flesh and happy.

" 'The old woman, a resident of the mountain resort town for ninety-seven years, called this office to report her observation. Local residents report that Mrs. Fielder is a fine old member of the community, who only occasionally sees imaginary things.' "

Bando roared. I must say I was sweating, for I really did not expect this turn of events.

"And now," went on Bando, "and now the queen of the New York papers. This story was buried on page nineteen. No sensationalism for this paper."

(1) Why do officials claim that the boy doesn't exist?

Officials say there is no evidence of a boy living alone in the mountains because all

_____

for such events.

(2) How does Mrs. Fielder describe the boy's appearance and mood?

She describes the boy as _____, dusty, in _____ and happy.

(3) What description of Mrs. Fielder calls into question her reliability?

The paper says that local residents report that she only _____

_____.

(4) Compare the reactions of Bando and the boy to the news article.

Bando _____, but the boy was _____.

Read the passage. Then answer the questions below using words from the passage.

BOY REPORTED LIVING OFF LAND IN CATSKILLS

" 'A young boy of seventeen or eighteen, who left home with a group of boy scouts, is reported to be still scouting in that area, according to the fire warden of the Catskill Mountains.

" 'Evidence of someone living in the forest — a fireplace, soup bones, and cracked nuts — was reported by Warden Jim Handy, who spent the night in the wilderness looking for the lad. Jim stated that the young man had apparently left the area, as there was no evidence of his camp upon a second trip — ' "

"What second trip?" I asked.

Bando puffed his pipe, looked at me wistfully* and said, "Are you ready to listen?"

"Sure," I answered.

"Well, here's the rest of it. '…there was no trace of his camp on a second trip, and the warden believes that the young man returned to his home at the end of the summer.'

"You know, Thoreau, I could scarcely drag myself away from the newspapers to come up here. You make a marvelous story."

…

I gave Bando his presents when he returned. He liked them. He was really pleased; I could tell by his eyebrows. They went up and down and in and out. Furthermore, I know he liked the presents because he wore them.

The onion soup was about to be served when I heard a voice shouting in the distance, "I know you are there! I know you are there! Where are you?"

*wistful – described by wishful yearning; sad, melancholy

(1) About how old is the boy reported to be?

The boy is reported to be _____.

(2) What evidence did the warden see of someone living in the forest?

The warden saw _____.

(3) What did Bando say about the newspapers?

Bando said that he could _____ himself _____

_____ because the boy made _____.

(4) How did the boy know that Bando liked his presents?

The boy knew that Bando liked his presents because his eyebrows went _____

_____ and because he _____.

The wild boy is famous!
Would you like to be in the newspapers like him?

Reading Comprehension
My Side of the Mountain 4

Level ★★★

30

Date   /   /

Name

Score

/100

1 Read the passage. Then answer the questions below using words from the passage.

10 points per question

"*Dad*!" I screamed, and dove right through the door onto my stomach. I all but fell down the mountain shouting, "Dad! Dad! Where are you?" I found him resting in a snowdrift, looking at the cardinal pair that lived near the stream. He was smiling, stretched out on his back, not in exhaustion, but in joy.

"Merry Christmas!" he whooped. I ran toward him. He jumped to his feet, tackled me, thumped my chest, and rubbed snow in my face.

Then he stood up, lifted me from the snow by the pockets on my coat, and held me off the ground so that we were eye to eye. He sure smiled. He threw me down in the snow again and wrestled with me for a few minutes. Our formal greeting done, we strode up to the mountain.

"Well, son," he began. "I've been reading about you in the papers and I could no longer resist the temptation to visit you. I still can't believe you did it."

His arm went around me. He looked real good, and I was overjoyed to see him.

"How did you find me?" I asked eagerly.

"I went to Mrs. Fielder, and she told me which mountain. At the stream I found your raft and ice-fishing holes. Then I looked for trails and footsteps. When I thought I was getting warm, I hollered."

"Am I that easy to find?"

"You didn't have to answer, and I'd probably have frozen in the snow." He was pleased and not angry at me at all.

(1) Upon hearing his father's voice, what did the boy do to show his excitement?

The boy screamed and _____ onto his stomach.

(2) What was the father doing that suggested he enjoyed nature?

The father was resting _____ and looking at _____

_____ that lived near the stream.

(3) How did the father greet the boy?

The father whooped, _____ the boy, _____ the boy's chest,

_____ in the boy's face, and held him _____

the pockets on his coat so that they were _____. Then he smiled and

_____ with the boy for a few minutes.

(4) How did the boy feel about being found by his father?

The boy was _____ to see his father and _____ asked how his
father found him.

2 Read the passage. Then answer the questions below.

12 points per question

He said again, "I just didn't think you'd do it. I was sure you'd be back the next day. When you weren't, I bet on the next week; then the next month. How's it going?"

"Oh, it's a wonderful life, Dad!"

When we walked into the tree, Bando was putting the final touches on the venison steak.

"Dad, this is my friend, Professor Bando; he's a teacher. He got lost one day last summer and stumbled onto my camp. He liked it so well that he came back for Christmas. Bando, meet my father."

Bando turned the steak on the spit, rose, and shook my father's hand.

"I am pleased to meet the man who sired this boy," he said grandly. I could see that they liked each other and that it was going to be a splendid Christmas. Dad stretched out on the bed and looked around.

"I thought maybe you'd pick a cave," he said. "The papers reported that they were looking for you in old sheds and houses, but I knew better than that. However, I never would have thought of the inside of a tree. What a beauty! Very clever, son, very, very clever. This is a comfortable bed."

He noticed my food caches, stood and peered into them. "Got enough to last until spring?"

"I think so," I said. "If I don't keep getting hungry visitors all the time." I winked at him.

"Well, I would wear out my welcome by a year if I could, but I have to get back to work soon after Christmas."

(1) Was the father surprised that the boy had made it for so long?

_____, the father seemed surprised at first because he was sure that his son would

be back _____.

(2) How did the boy feel about living alone in the wilderness?

The boy thought it was _____.

(3) How did the boy meet Bando?

The boy met Bando when the professor _____ in the

summer and _____ his camp.

(4) Why did the boy think it would be a splendid Christmas?

The boy thought it would be a splendid Christmas because Bando and his father _____

_____.

(5) How confident did the boy seem about supporting himself in the wilderness?

The boy seemed confident about supporting himself in the

wilderness because he _____ his father when

he was asked about his food.

What do you think
will happen next?

Reading Comprehension
The Red Pony 1

31

Level
★★★

Date / /

Name

Score

/100

1 Read the following text from *The Red Pony* by John Steinbeck, in which the ranch-hand Billy Buck and ranch owner Carl Tiflin give a horse to Carl's 10-year-old son, Jody. Then fill in the charts below according to the passage. 25 points per question

A red pony colt was looking at him out of the stall. Its tense ears were forward and a light of disobedience was in its eyes. Its coat was rough and thick as an Airedale's fur and its mane was long and tangled. Jody's throat collapsed in on itself and cut his breath short.

"He needs a good currying," his father said, "and if I ever hear of you not feeding him or leaving his stall dirty, I'll sell him off in a minute."

Jody couldn't bear to look at the pony's eyes any more. He gazed down at his hands for a moment, and he asked very shyly, "Mine?" No one answered him. He put his hand out toward the pony. Its gray nose came close, sniffing loudly, and then the lips drew back and the strong teeth closed on Jody's fingers. The pony shook its head up and down and seemed to laugh with amusement. Jody regarded his bruised fingers. "Well," he said with pride — "Well, I guess he can bite all right." The two men laughed, somewhat in relief. Carl Tiflin went out of the barn and walked up a side-hill to be by himself, for he was embarrassed, but Billy Buck stayed. It was easier to talk to Billy Buck. Jody asked again — "Mine?"

Billy became professional in tone. "Sure! That is, if you look out for him and break him right. I'll show you how. He's just a colt. You can't ride him for some time."

(1) Fill in the chart to describe the red pony.

Description of the Pony
Its ①_____ ears were ②_____.
A ③_____ was in its eyes.
Its coat was ④_____ as an Airedale's fur.
Its mane was ⑤_____.

(2) Fill in the chart listing the actions of the pony after Jody first puts his hand out.

Actions of the Pony
Its gray nose ①_____, _____ loudly.
Its lips ②_____.
The strong teeth ③_____.
It shook its head ④_____ and seemed to
⑤_____.

"The Gift", from THE RED PONY by John Steinbeck, copyright 1933, 1937, 1938 © renewed 1961, 1965, 1966 by John Steinbeck. Used by permission of Viking Penguin, a division of Penguin Group (USA) Inc.

2 Read the passage. Then answer the questions below using words from the passage.

10 points per question

Jody put out his bruised hand again, and this time the red pony let his nose be rubbed. "I ought to have a carrot," Jody said. "Where'd we get him, Billy?"

"Bought him at a sheriff's auction," Billy explained. "A show went broke in Salinas and had debts. The sheriff was selling off their stuff."

The pony stretched out his nose and shook the forelock from his wild eyes. Jody stroked the nose a little. He said softly, "There isn't a — saddle?"

Billy Buck laughed. "I'd forgot. Come along."

In the harness room he lifted down a little saddle of red morocco leather. "It's just a show saddle," Billy Buck said disparagingly*. "It isn't practical* for the brush, but it was cheap at the sale."

Jody couldn't trust himself to look at the saddle either, and he couldn't speak at all. He brushed the shining red leather with his fingertips, and after a long time he said, "It'll look pretty on him though." He thought of the grandest and prettiest things he knew. "If he hasn't a name already, I think I'll call him Gabilan Mountains," he said.

Billy Buck knew how he felt. "It's a pretty long name. Why don't you just call him Gabilan? That means hawk. That would be a fine name for him." Billy felt glad. "If you will collect tail hair, I might be able to make a hair rope for you sometime. You could use it for a hackamore*."

*disparagingly – to speak badly about / *practical – useful / *hackamore – a special kind of bridle, or headgear for a horse

(1) When did the pony let Jody rub his nose?

The pony let Jody rub his nose after he _____

_____ .

(2) How did Billy Buck describe the red morocco leather saddle?

Billy said that it was just _____ that wasn't _____

_____ , but it was _____ .

(3) How did Jody react to the saddle?

Jody couldn't _____ , and

he couldn't _____ , but he did brush _____

_____ .

(4) How did Jody think of a name for the red pony?

Jody thought of _____ he knew.

(5) What did Billy think about the name Jody chose?

Billy knew _____ and thought

Gabilan would be _____ for
the horse.

Have you ever gotten
on a horse?

Reading Comprehension
The Red Pony 2

32

Level ★★★

Date   /   /

Name

Score   /100

1   Read the passage. Then answer the questions below using words from the passage.

10 points per question

Jody wanted to go back to the box stall. "Could I lead him to school, do you think — to show the kids?"

But Billy shook his head. "He's not even halter-broke yet. We had a time getting him here. Had to almost drag him. You better be starting for school though."

"I'll bring the kids to see him here this afternoon," Jody said.

Six boys came over the hill half an hour early that afternoon, running hard, their heads down, their forearms working, their breath whistling. They swept by the house and cut across the stubble-field to the barn. And then they stood self-consciously before the pony, and then they looked at Jody with eyes in which there was a new admiration and a new respect. Before today Jody had been a boy, dressed in overalls and a blue shirt — quieter than most, even suspected of being a little cowardly. And now he was different. Out of a thousand centuries they drew the ancient admiration of the footman for the horseman. They knew instinctively that a man on a horse is spiritually as well as physically bigger than a man on foot. They knew that Jody had been miraculously lifted out of equality with them, and had been placed over them. Gabilan put his head out of the stall and sniffed them.

"Why'n't you ride him?" the boys cried. "Why'n't you braid his tail with ribbons like in the fair?" "When you going to ride him?"

(1) What did Jody ask Billy?

Jody asked Billy if he could _____ the pony _____ to _____

_____.

(2) Describe how the six boys approached the barn.

The boys ran _____

_____ whistling.

(3) How did the boys look at Jody?

The boys looked at Jody with eyes in which there was a new _____

_____.

(4) What did the boys know instinctively?

They knew instinctively _____

_____ than a man on foot.

(5) What did the boys know had miraculously happened to Jody?

They knew that Jody had been miraculously _____

_____.

Read the passage. Then answer the questions below using words from the passage.

Jody's courage was up. He too felt the superiority of the horseman. "He's not old enough. Nobody can ride him for a long time. I'm going to train him on the long halter. Billy Buck is going to show me how."

"Well, can't we even lead him around a little?"

"He isn't even halter-broke," Jody said. He wanted to be completely alone when he took the pony out for the first time. "Come and see the saddle."

They were speechless at the red morocco saddle, completely shocked out of comment. "It isn't much use in the brush," Jody explained. "It'll look pretty on him though. Maybe I'll ride bareback when I go into the brush."

"How you going to rope a cow without a saddle horn?"

"Maybe I'll get another saddle for every day. My father might want me to help him with the stock." He let them feel the red saddle, and showed them the brass chain throat-latch on the bridle and the big brass buttons at each temple where the headstall and brow band crossed. The whole thing was too wonderful. They had to go away after a little while, and each boy, in his mind, searched among his possessions for a bribe worthy of offering in return for a ride on the red pony when the time should come.

Jody was glad when they had gone. He took brush and currycomb from the wall, took down the barrier of the box stall and stepped cautiously in.

(1) Why was Jody's courage up?

His courage was up because he too felt the _____.

(2) How did Jody respond when the boys asked to lead the horse around a little?

Jody said that the horse wasn't even _____.

(3) Why didn't Jody want to take the pony out with the boys?

Jody wanted to be completely _____ took _____

_____.

(4) How did the boys respond to seeing the red morocco saddle?

They were _____ and completely _____,
just as Jody was when he first saw it.

(5) What did the boys think about when they had to leave?

Each boy, in his mind, searched _____

_____

_____

_____ when the time should come.

If I were Jody,
I wouldn't be so patient!

Reading Comprehension
The Red Pony 3

33

Level ★★★

Score

Date / /

Name

/ 100

1 Read the passage. Then answer the questions below using words from the passage.

12 points per question

> The pony's eyes glittered, and he edged around into kicking position. But Jody touched him on the shoulder and rubbed his high arched neck as he had always seen Billy Buck do, and he crooned, "So-o-o, boy," in a deep voice. The pony gradually relaxed his tenseness. Jody curried and brushed until a pile of dead hair lay in the stall and until the pony's coat had taken on a deep red shine. Each time he finished he thought it might have been done better. He braided the mane into a dozen little pigtails, and he braided the forelock, and then he undid them and brushed the hair out straight again.
>
> Jody did not hear his mother enter the barn. She was angry when she came, but when she looked in at the pony and at Jody working over him, she felt a curious pride rise up in her. "Have you forgot the wood-box?" she asked gently. "It's not far off from dark and there's not a stick of wood in the house, and the chickens aren't fed."
>
> Jody quickly put up his tools. "I forgot, ma'am."
>
> "Well, after this do your chores first. Then you won't forget. I expect you'll forget lots of things now if I don't keep an eye on you."
>
> "Can I have carrots from the garden for him, ma'am?"
>
> She had to think about that. "Oh — I guess so, if you only take the big tough ones."
>
> "Carrots keep the coat good," he said, and again she felt the curious rush of pride.

(1) What caused the pony to gradually relax its tenseness?

The pony gradually relaxed after Jody _____

and _____ as he had seen Billy Buck do.

(2) How long did Jody curry and brush the horse's hair?

Jody curried and brushed the horse's hair until _____

_____ and until _____

_____.

(3) How did Jody feel when he finished currying and brushing the horse's hair?

Each time he finished he thought it _____.

(4) Why was Jody's mother angry at first?

She was angry because there was not _____ in the house and

the chickens weren't _____.

(5) When did the mother feel a curious rush of pride?

She felt a curious rush of pride when she looked _____

_____ the pony and again when Jody explained that,

" _____."

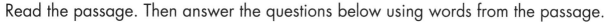

2 Read the passage. Then answer the questions below using words from the passage.

10 points per question

Jody never waited for the triangle to get him out of bed after the coming of the pony. It became his habit to creep out of bed even before his mother was awake, to slip into his clothes and to go quietly down to the barn to see Gabilan. In the gray quiet mornings when the land and the brush and the houses and the trees were silver-gray and black like a photograph negative, he stole toward the barn, past the sleeping stones and the sleeping cypress tree. The turkeys, roosting in the tree out of coyotes' reach, clicked drowsily. The fields glowed with a gray frost-like light and in the dew the tracks of rabbits and of field mice stood out sharply. The good dogs came stiffly out of their little houses, hackles* up and deep growls in their throats. Then they caught Jody's scent, and their stiff tails rose up and waved a greeting — Doubletree Mutt with the big thick tail, and Smasher, the incipient* shepherd — then went lazily back to their warm beds.

It was a strange time and a mysterious journey, to Jody — an extension of a dream. When he first had the pony he liked to torture himself during the trip by thinking Gabilan would not be in his stall, and worse, would never have been there. And he had other delicious little self-induced pains. He thought how the rats had gnawed ragged holes in the red saddle, and how the mice had nibbled Gabilan's tail until it was stringy and thin.

hackles – hair along neck / *incipient* – coming into being

(1) How did Jody change after the coming of the pony?

Jody _____

_____ after the coming of the pony.

(2) Fill in the chart to describe the gray quiet mornings when Jody would slip into his clothes to see his horse.

The gray quiet mornings
The land and the brush and the houses and trees were silver-gray and black like a ①_____, the ②_____ and the ③_____ were sleeping, the fields ④_____, and in the dew ⑤_____ stood out sharply.

(3) What kind of time was this for Jody?

It was a _____ and a _____ — an _____ of _____.

(4) What did Jody like to do during the trip to the barn?

He liked to _____ during the

trip by thinking _____

_____.

What a beautiful description!

Reading Comprehension

The Red Pony 4

34

Score

/100

Date / /

Name

---

1 Read the passage. Then answer the questions below using words from the passage.

15 points per question

> He usually ran the last little way to the barn. He unlatched the rusty hasp* of the barn door and stepped in, and no matter how quietly he opened the door, Gabilan was always looking at him over the barrier of the box stall and Gabilan whinnied softly and stamped his front foot, and his eyes had big sparks of red fire in them like oakwood embers.
>
> Sometimes, if the work horses were to be used that day, Jody found Billy Buck in the barn harnessing and currying. Billy stood with him and looked long at Gabilan and he told Jody a great many things about horses. He explained that they were terribly afraid for their feet, so that one must make a practice of lifting the legs and patting the hoofs and ankles to remove their terror. He told Jody how horses love conversation. He must talk to the pony all the time, and tell him the reasons for everything. Billy wasn't sure a horse could understand everything that was said to him, but it was impossible to say how much was understood. A horse never kicked up a fuss if some one he liked explained things to him. Billy could give examples, too. He had known, for instance, a horse nearly dead beat with fatigue to perk up when told it was only a little farther to his destination. And he had known a horse paralyzed with fright to come out of it when his rider told him what it was that was frightening him.

hasp – a fastener for a door

(1) Describe what Gabilan always did and what his eyes looked like when Jody opened the door.

Gabilan always looked _____ the box stall,

_____ softly, _____ foot, and his eyes had

_____ like oakwood embers.

(2) Fill in the chart below about the second paragraph.

Main Idea	Billy tells Jody a great ①_____.
Supporting Details	Horses are terribly ②_____.
	Horses love ③_____.

(3) As a result of horses being terribly afraid for their feet, what must one do?

One must make a practice of _____

_____.

(4) As a result of horses loving conversation, what does Billy tell Jody he must do?

Jody must _____, and _____

_____.

 © Kumon Publishing Co., Ltd.

Read the passage. Then answer the questions below using words from the passage.

8 points per question

While he talked in the mornings, Billy Buck cut twenty or thirty straws into neat three-inch lengths and stuck them into his hatband. Then during the whole day, if he wanted to pick his teeth or merely to chew on something, he had only to reach up for one of them.

Jody listened carefully, for he knew and the whole county knew that Billy Buck was a fine hand with horses. Billy's own horse was a stringy cayuse with a hammer head, but he nearly always won first prize at the stock trials. Billy could rope a steer, take a double half-hitch about the horn with his riata*, and dismount, and his horse would play the steer as an angler plays a fish, keeping a tight rope until the steer was down or beaten.

Every morning, after Jody had curried and brushed the pony, he let down the barrier of the stall, and Gabilan thrust past him and raced down the barn and into the corral. Around and around he galloped, and sometimes he jumped forward and landed on stiff legs. He stood quivering, stiff ears forward, eyes rolling so that the whites showed, pretending to be frightened. At last he walked snorting to the water-trough and buried his nose in the water up to the nostrils. Jody was proud then, for he knew that was the way to judge a horse. Poor horses only touched their lips to the water, but a fine spirited beast put his whole nose and mouth under, and only left room to breathe.

*riata – lasso

(1) Describe what Billy Buck did while he talked in the mornings, and why he did this.

While he talked, _____

_____

_____ so that during the whole day he would have something to _____

_____ or merely _____.

(2) What is the main idea of the second paragraph?

Jody listened carefully, _____

_____.

(3) Describe what Gabilan did every morning in the corral.

Every morning, Gabilan galloped _____, then he stood _____

_____

_____ and pretended to be frightened.

(4) How did Gabilan drink water?

Gabilan buried _____.

(5) Why did that make Jody proud?

Jody was proud because he knew _____

_____, and that a fine

spirited beast like him would put _____

_____, leaving only

_____.

I want to know more about this horse!

1 Read the following passage. Complete the passage using the vocabulary words defined below.

5 points per question

You can probably name at least one famous person, perhaps an athlete, movie star, or a historical (1)_____ whom you learned about at school. Famous people can be known for a special (2)_____, such as an invention or a new world record. Artists have gained (3)_____ by creating works that (4)_____ to many people. Famous people such as athletes often become positive (5)_____ to young people who want to be just like them. The life stories of famous people often give us (6)_____ to try harder.

achievement(s)	something gained or reached by effort
inspiration	a feeling of encouragement from someone or something
appeal	to be interesting or enjoyable
role model(s)	someone admired and imitated
figure	a well-known person
recognition	favorable attention

2 Read the passage. Then complete the main idea for each paragraph in the chart below.

10 points per question

Tarzan is a well-known fictional character. The jungle hero first appeared in a magazine story by Edgar Rice Burroughs. The first Tarzan novel, *Tarzan of the Apes*, was followed by several sequels.*

The jungle adventures of Tarzan have fascinated readers for many years. The novel begins with Tarzan, the son of an English lord, being left behind as a baby in the jungles of Africa. Tarzan is adopted and raised by a troop of great apes.

The story of Tarzan has been told in many forms. The first movie version was a silent film. Tarzan has also been the hero of a comic strip and several more modern movies.

*sequel(s) – a story that continues an earlier story

Main Idea	Tarzan is a famous (1)_____.
	⬇
	Readers have long enjoyed the (2)_____.
	⬇
	The Tarzan story (3)_____.

3 Complete the crossword puzzle using the sentences below as clues. Use capital letters.

5 points per question

The crossword grid contains the following pre-filled letters:

(7) column: A, M, Y
(1) row: P, F, S
(5) row
(2) row: D, M ... Y
(6) row: C
... C
... V
(3) row: C, G ... N
(8) column: V, N
(4) row: G, N ... T

ACROSS

(1) ___?___ athletes make a lot of money.

(2) At the last second, the hockey puck ___?___ slid into the goal.

(3) When he finally saw who I was under my mask, I could see a wave of ___?___ go across his face.

(4) The Grand Canyon offers some ___?___ views.

DOWN

(5) I've always expressed my ___?___ for teachers and the work they do.

(6) James was happy because it was a great ___?___ to win a science award.

(7) I like to wander ___?___ around at the mall. I don't usually have a shopping list.

(8) Caroline didn't really like the taste of ___?___ steak.

Almost there!

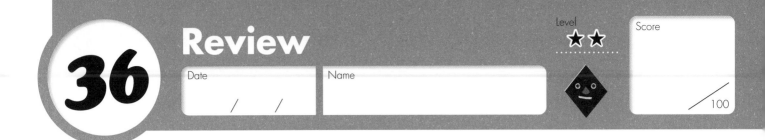

1 Read the passage. Then complete the chart below.

5 points per question

> Robin Hood is a legendary hero, whose existence as a real living man is still not confirmed. His name first appears in a group of English songs, some of which date from the 14th century. These old songs tell the story of Robin Hood and his band of followers in the Sherwood Forest near Nottingham. Inside the forest, they shot at targets with bows and arrows, hunted the king's deer, robbed from the rich, and gave to the poor.
>
> The legend of Robin Hood describes the cruelty* of life during the 14th century and the harsh laws for the average person. Robin Hood has become a symbol of liberty. He stands for the rights of the people against unfair laws.

*cruelty – inhuman treatment

Main Idea	Robin Hood was a hero.
Supporting Details	He robbed from the rich, and (1)_____. He is a symbol (2)_____. He stands for (3)_____ _____.

2 Read the passage. Then complete the chart below.

5 points per question

> Alexander Graham Bell's mother and wife were both deaf, so he spent much of his life trying to help the deaf. His father also taught deaf people how to make words and read lips. Even as a young man, Bell was interested in the sound of the human voice and how the ear hears it. This background led him to invent the telephone in 1876.
>
> In addition to the telephone, Mr. Bell invented the audiometer, a device that measures the power of sound. He also helped educate the deaf through his institutions: The Volta Laboratory and the Alexander Graham Bell Association for the Deaf.

General Causes	General Effects
Mr. Bell's mother and wife (1)_____ _____.	Mr. Bell spent much of his life (4)_____ _____.
Mr. Bell's father taught (2)_____ _____ and (3)_____.	Mr. Bell invented (5)_____ and the (6)_____ and helped (7)_____ the deaf through his institutions.

© Kumon Publishing Co., Ltd.

3 Read the passage. Then complete the chart about Anne in *Anne of Green Gables* below.

4 points per question

Lucy Maud Montgomery, a Canadian author born in 1874, was the creator of Anne Shirley, the beloved character of *Anne of Green Gables*. The book tells the story of how a spirited and talkative orphan changes the lives of an elderly brother and sister. It has six sequels that follow Anne through childhood to adulthood.

Due to her rebellious nature, Anne often comes into conflict with the rules of the society in which she lived, and her red hair is a symbol of her restless energy.

These characteristics make her very popular among young readers, who can also relate to her optimism and vivid* imagination. Since her fictional birth, Anne has inspired many productions on the stage, screen and television.

*vivid – active, sharp, intense

Descriptions of Anne	Results of Anne's Actions
Anne is a beloved character.	She changes the lives of an (4)_____
She is a (1)_____ orphan.	_____.
She has a (2)_____ nature.	She comes into (5)_____
She has (3)_____ and a vivid imagination.	_____ the rules of her society.

4 Read the passage. Then answer the questions.

10 points per question

Helen Keller is famous for her achievements, especially because of the overwhelming obstacles that she faced. A terrible illness left Helen deaf and blind. Because she was under two years old when she lost her hearing, she did not learn to speak. When Keller was six years old, her parents took her to see Alexander Graham Bell. At his suggestion, a woman named Anne Sullivan became Keller's teacher. She taught Keller to read and write *braille*, a special alphabet for blind people. Keller eventually learned to speak as well.

Helen graduated from Radcliffe College in 1904. She later helped to found an institution called the Massachusetts Commission for the Blind. As a writer and lecturer, she helped people understand what life is like for the deaf and blind.

(1) What was Helen Keller's biggest obstacle?

Helen Keller's biggest obstacle was the fact that a terrible _____ her

_____.

(2) What alphabet did Anne Sullivan teach Helen Keller?

Anne Sullivan taught Keller _____, a special _____

_____.

(3) What did Helen Keller help people understand?

Helen Keller _____

_____.

Congratulations!
You did it!

© Kumon Publishing Co., Ltd. 73

1 Vocabulary
pp 2, 3

1 (1) ① diverse ② delicious
③ densely ④ rural
(2) ① to an apartment building in Chicago
② to give so many people a place to live
③ enough sunlight for the plants

2 (1) the most delicious vegetables
(2) densely placed gardening plots
(3) some people grow vegetables
(4) keep the air clean / building cooler during warmer
(5) more rural areas

2 Vocabulary
pp 4, 5

1 (1) ① campaign ② debates
③ election ④ politics
⑤ candidate
(2) ① passes out brochures
② run for president

2 (1) silly to spend the class money on an ice cream day
(2) to the other kids and make good choices for them
(3) the president listen / ideas
(4) to be treasurer / in charge of the class money

3 Vocabulary
pp 6, 7

1 (1) ① legend ② habitat
③ glimpsed ④ captured
⑤ gigantic ⑥ limbs
⑦ elongated
(2) ① sea monster that attacked ships
② adult giant squid
③ in the stomachs of the sperm whales

2 (1) most of the earth's oceans
(2) did not survive
(3) eyes the size of volleyballs / the light of other ocean life to see
(4) first glimpse of the giant squid / natural habitat
(5) the total length of the squid

4 Vocabulary
pp 8, 9

1 (1) ① brief ② athletic
③ resembles ④ example
(2) ① Soccer and volleyball are played in the United States
② outside / use balls instead of pins
③ called cricket
④ began as a children's game

2 (1) resembles hockey
(2) long sticks with heads shaped like hammers
(3) on horseback
(4) the other team's kite to the ground
(5) very brief / as long as an hour
(6) twist / modern games

5 Vocabulary Review
pp 10, 11

1 (1) rural (2) legends
(3) captured (4) elections
(5) limb

2 (1) ⓒ (2) ⓕ
(3) ⓑ (4) ⓔ
(5) ⓐ (6) ⓓ

3 (1) RESEMBLED
(2) BRIEF
(3) GLIMPSED
(4) ATHLETIC
(5) DENSELY
(6) CAMPAIGNS
(7) DEBATES
(8) ELONGATED

6 Main Idea & Supporting Elements
pp 12, 13

1 (1) ⓒ
(2) ⓓ

2 (1) ⓑ
(2) ⓐ
(3) ⓐ

7 Main Idea & Supporting Elements pp 14,15

1 (1) ① the stars
② compass
③ magnets
④ making pictures
⑤ location
(2) ⓐ

2 (1) ① more detailed and correct
② science
③ pictures
④ show what a place is like
(2) ⓐ

8 Main Idea & Supporting Elements pp 16,17

1 (1) ① wind blow
② air
③ source of power
④ use wind power
(2) ⓑ

2 (1) ① crushed the grain
② pumps
③ moved
④ transform
⑤ water
⑥ convert
⑦ electricity
(2) ⓒ

9 Main Idea & Supporting Elements pp 18,19

1 (1) declined
(2) ⓑ

2 (1) ① places that are very windy
② Ocean winds
③ buildings or trees to
(2) ① their problems
② a lot of space
③ hazards like storms and ice

10 Main Idea & Supporting Elements pp 20,21

1 (1) ① B   ② C   ③ A
(2) ⓒ

2 (1) ⓐ
(2) ① A   ② C   ③ B
(3) ① wooden boat buried
② sent to search behind a sealed door

11 Vocabulary Review pp 22,23

1 (1) dramatic
(2) scale
(3) civilizations
(4) declined
(5) delivered
(6) landmark

2 (1) free
(2) changes
(3) dig
(4) spot

3 (1) RELIABLE
(2) IMPROVED
(3) COMMUNICATION
(4) CLIMATE
(5) PYRAMIDS
(6) EFFECTIVE
(7) IMAGINATIVE
(8) MECHANICAL

12 Cause & Effect pp 24,25

1 (1) bright sun and nearly cloudless sky
(2) raked the yard that week
(3) swum in the lake and picked blackberries
(4) hear the pouring rain hitting
(5) wouldn't go to Turboworld at all

2 (1) how slowly / eating breakfast
(2) description of the Twisting Falls of Horror
(3) preferred to stay on solid ground
(4) she had to finish her breakfast before
(5) help convincing Val to ride

13 Cause & Effect

1 (1) already been postponed
  (2) ① right-side up
    ② really liked heights
    ③ Racing Turbo Beetles
    ④ Bouncing Bumper Cars

2 (1) actually waterfalls that pass through caves
  (2) give the car its speed
  (3) for having been so disagreeable before
  (4) ① screamed with glee
    ② Jeremy's pale face

14 Cause & Effect
pp 28,29

1 (1) arranged for the family to get rides on the tractor
  (2) the weather would be the same as it always was
  (3) busy with work / talking on the phone
  (4) was now coming down steadily / it was cold
  (5) tractor got stuck / budge

2 (1) ① ran out of gas
    ② developed a cold
  (2) huddle
  (3) around in the cold rain / coat
  (4) apple turnovers / breakfast

15 Cause & Effect
pp 30,31

1 (1) ① precautions   ② procedure(s)
    ③ hazards   ④ supervise
    ⑤ conflict   ⑥ violence

2 (1) not taking simple precautions
  (2) Common activities / crossing a street, eating food, or playing sports
  (3) people follow them properly

3 (1) carelessness
  (2) tables and chairs as ladders / kitchen appliances
  (3) left on steps / Spilled water
  (4) unfamiliar with these places / public places are often crowded

16 Vocabulary Review
pp 32,33

1 (1) demanded
  (2) precaution
  (3) convince
  (4) conflict
  (5) budge
  (6) develop

2 (1) ⓔ
  (2) ⓓ
  (3) ⓐ
  (4) ⓑ
  (5) ⓒ

3 (1) COLOSSAL
  (2) DISAGREEABLE
  (3) POSTPONED
  (4) CURVE
  (5) EXPLAINED
  (6) OPPOSED
  (7) ARRANGED
  (8) FLICKER

17 Actions & Descriptions
pp 34,35

1 (1) short spiky brown hair / a round face
  (2) went on his first camping trip
  (3) ⓐ, ⓒ

2 (1) ⓒ, ⓓ, ⓔ
  (2) his compass and found north using
  (3) start a fire

18 Actions & Descriptions
pp 36,37

1 (1) ⓐ, ⓓ, ⓖ
  (2) ⓐ 2 ⓑ 1 ⓒ 3 ⓓ 5 ⓔ 4

2 (1) open another energy bar / ate it quickly
  (2) huddled / the fire
  (3) struggled / the poles
  (4) racket out beyond his fire
  (5) happy to see

 © Kumon Publishing Co., Ltd.

19 Actions & Descriptions pp 38,39

1 (1) ① played the same sport
  ② worked hard to be better than the other
  ③ two seeds in different conditions
  ④ (then) compare the results
(2) ⓑ, ⓓ

2 (1) excited
(2) raced to their rooms
(3) talkative twin
(4) talking, singing, and dancing
(5) talked to it
(6) danced around the room with it
(7) quieter than her sister
(8) write stories
(9) wrote a story about growing big and tall
(10) whispered the story to her plant

20 Actions & Descriptions pp 40,41

1 (1) ① very friendly girls
  ② groaned at her mother
  ③ ran back up to her room
(2) groaned and ran upstairs like her sister

2 (1) ⓑ, ⓒ, ⓓ, ⓕ
(2) on the same team / proud / working together

21 Vocabulary Reviw pp 42,43

1 (1) wildlife   (2) eventually
(3) opposed   (4) boulder
(5) compass

2 (1) ⓓ   (2) ⓔ
(3) ⓐ   (4) ⓕ
(5) ⓒ   (6) ⓑ

3 (1) RIDICULOUS
(2) PATIENT
(3) EXCLAIMED
(4) WILDERNESS
(5) TINDER
(6) RACKET
(7) CULTIVATE
(8) JOURNAL

22 Characters pp 44,45

1 (1) very tired of sitting by her sister on the bank /
  having nothing to do
(2) very sleepy and stupid
(3) A White Rabbit / pink eyes
(4) a watch out of its waistcoat-pocket

2 (1) ten inches high
(2) if she was going to shrink any further
(3) the little golden key / she could not possibly reach it
(4) sat down and cried
(5) sharply / crying

23 Characters pp 46,47

1 (1) ① very good advice
  ② having cheated herself in a game
(2) she remained the same size
(3) expecting nothing / dull and stupid for life to go on
  in the common way

2 (1) more than nine feet high
(2) more hopeless than ever
(3) ought to be ashamed of herself
(4) splendidly dressed / pair of white kid gloves in one
  hand / large fan in the other
(5) trotting along in a great hurry / to himself

24 Characters pp 48,49

1 (1) started violently / the white kid gloves and the fan /
  scurried away
(2) changed in the night
(3) not the same / in the world
(4) ① goes in such long ringlets
  ② Mabel

2 (1) busily painting / red
(2) splashing paint over
(3) cook tulip-roots instead of onions
(4) white one in by mistake

25 Characters   pp 50,51

1 (1) carrying
(2) the three gardeners
(3) ornamented all over
(4) jumping merrily along hand in hand
(5) guests
(6) the King's crown
(7) a crimson velvet cushion
(8) King and Queen of Hearts

2 (1) remember ever having heard of such a rule at /
to lie down upon their faces / that they couldn't see
it
(2) very politely
(3) on their backs was the same as the rest of the pack
(4) courage / no business
(5) loudly and decidedly / nonsense

26 Vocabulary Review   pp 52,53

1 (1) waistcoat   (2) script
(3) courtiers   (4) resources
(5) represent   (6) convert

2 (1) quickly   (2) confusing
(3) march   (4) decorated

3 (1) TELESCOPE
(2) THEATRICAL
(3) EXPECTING
(4) SHEDDING
(5) RESPECTABLE
(6) REMARKABLE
(7) ALTOGETHER
(8) SPLENDIDLY

27 Reading Comprehension   pp 54,55

1 (1) to bed early / late / mountain harvest
(2) It was very, very nice
(3) breath froze in his nostrils / body was snug and
comfortable
(4) come back / fist with a thump and a flip
(5) read so much about the loneliness / farmer, the
trapper / the woodsman / bleakness of winter /
come to believe it

2 (1) chasing the young chickadees through the woods
(2) noisy, scolding / busily following each other
(3) ① followed Mrs. O'Brien
② followed Mrs. Callaway
③ flit and rush
④ click and fly from one eating spot

28 Reading Comprehension   pp 56,57

1 (1) quiet as the apartment house on Third Avenue /
were off the streets / had said their last words to
each
(2) for only a few hours / whether or not it was too
stormy for good hunting / disappear
(3) who more enjoyed doing nothing on a bad day than
Mr. Bracket of Third Avenue
(4) sleet and snow drove down / all holed up

2 (1) living off deer and nuts / wilderness
(2) wounded and couldn't find
(3) their wives / came home without their deer
(4) red-blooded American boy / to live in a tree house
and trap his own food / do it

29 Reading Comprehension   pp 58,59

1 (1) abandoned houses and sheds are routinely
checked
(2) brown-haired / good flesh
(3) occasionally sees imaginary things
(4) roared / sweating

2 (1) seventeen or eighteen
(2) a fireplace, soup bones, and cracked nuts
(3) scarcely drag / away from the newspapers /
a marvelous story
(4) up and down and in and out / wore them

30 Reading Comprehension   pp 60,61

1 (1) dove right through the door
(2) in a snowdrift / the cardinal pair
(3) tackled / thumped / rubbed snow / by the pockets
on / eye to eye / wrestled
(4) overjoyed / eagerly

2 (1) Yes / the next day

(2) a wonderful life

(3) got lost one day / stumbled onto

(4) liked each other

(5) winked at

(31) Reading Comprehension pp 62,63

1 (1) ① tense

② forward

③ light of disobedience

④ rough and thick

⑤ long and tangled

(2) ① came close, sniffing

② drew back

③ closed on Jody's fingers

④ up and down

⑤ laugh with amusement

2 (1) put out his bruised hand again

(2) a show saddle / practical for the brush / cheap at the sale

(3) trust himself to look at the saddle / speak at all / the shining red leather with his fingertips

(4) the grandest and prettiest things

(5) how he felt / a fine name

(32) Reading Comprehension pp 64,65

1 (1) lead / to school / show the kids

(2) hard, their heads down, their forearms working, and their breath

(3) admiration and a new respect

(4) that a man on a horse is spiritually as well as physically bigger

(5) lifted out of equality with them, and had been placed over them

2 (1) superiority of the horseman

(2) halter-broke

(3) alone when he / the pony out for the first time

(4) speechless / shocked out of comment

(5) among his possessions for a bribe worthy of offering in return for a ride on the red pony

(33) Reading Comprehension pp 66,67

1 (1) touched him on the shoulder / rubbed his high arched neck

(2) a pile of dead hair lay in the stall / the pony's coat had taken on a deep red shine

(3) might have been done better

(4) a stick of wood / fed

(5) in at the pony and at Jody working over / Carrots keep the coat good

2 (1) never waited for the triangle to get him out of bed

(2) ① photograph negative

② stones

③ cypress tree

④ glowed with a gray frost-like light

⑤ the tracks of rabbits and of field mice

(3) strange time / mysterious journey / extension / a dream

(4) torture himself / Gabilan would not be in his stall

(34) Reading Comprehension pp 68,69

1 (1) at him over the barrier of / whinnied / stamped his front / big sparks of red fire in them

(2) ① many things about horses

② afraid for their feet

③ conversation

(3) lifting the legs and patting the hoofs and ankles to remove their terror

(4) talk to the pony all the time / tell him the reasons for everything

2 (1) Billy Buck cut twenty or thirty straws into neat three-inch lengths and stuck them into his hatband / pick his teeth / to chew on

(2) for he knew and the whole county knew that Billy Buck was a fine hand with horses

(3) around and around / quivering, stiff ears forward, eyes rolling so that the whites showed

(4) his nose in the water up to the nostrils

(5) that was the way to judge a horse / his whole nose and mouth under / room to breathe

(35) Review
pp 70,71

1 (1) figure
(2) achievement
(3) recognition
(4) appeal
(5) role models
(6) inspiration

2 (1) fictional character
(2) jungle adventures of Tarzan
(3) has been told in many forms

3 (1) PROFESSIONAL
(2) MIRACULOUSLY
(3) RECOGNITION
(4) MAGNIFICENT
(5) ADMIRATION
(6) ACHIEVEMENT
(7) AIMLESSLY
(8) VENISON

(36) Review
pp 72,73

1 (1) gave to the poor
(2) of liberty
(3) the rights of the people against unfair laws

2 (1) were both deaf
(2) deaf people how to make words
(3) read lips
(4) trying to help the deaf
(5) the telephone
(6) audiometer
(7) educate

3 (1) spirited and talkative
(2) rebellious
(3) optimism
(4) elderly brother and sister
(5) conflict with

4 (1) illness left / deaf and blind
(2) braille / alphabet for blind people
(3) helped people understand what life is like for the deaf and blind

 © Kumon Publishing Co., Ltd.